THE
PURITAN
FAMILY

THE PURITAN

HARPER TORCHBOOKS THE ACADEMY LIBRARY

*F*AMILY

Religion & Domestic Relations in Seventeenth-Century New England

EDMUND S. MORGAN

New Edition, Revised and Enlarged

HARPER & ROW, PUBLISHERS, NEW YORK

THE PURITAN FAMILY
Copyright © 1944, 1966
by Edmund Sears Morgan
Printed in the United States of America.

This book originally appeared
as part of *More Books,* the Bulletin
of the Boston Public Library, 1942-1943;
was published in book form by
the Public Library, Boston, in 1944 and 1956,
and was revised and expanded for the
Torchbook edition by the Author.

First HARPER TORCHBOOK edition
published 1966 by Harper & Row,
Publishers, Incorporated, New York

LIBRARY OF CONGRESS CATALOG
CARD NUMBER: 65-25695

99 98   RRD H   40 39 38 37 36

For
Helen
Penny
Pam

Contents

Foreword

*T*HIS book began as a dissertation in the history of American civilization at Harvard University, where it was presented for the degree in 1942. Most of the chapters in it were first published as articles in 1942 and 1943 in *More Books,* the bulletin of the Boston Public Library, edited by Zoltán Haraszti. In 1944 the articles were gathered into a book and published by the Boston Public Library under the present title. In 1956 the Library published a second edition, with minor corrections and alterations.

This new edition, published with the Library's kind permission, has been expanded in several ways. I have added a new opening chapter, which tries to place the Puritans' ideas about the family in the larger setting of their ideas about society and human relationships in general. I have also enlarged the discussion of this subject in chapter six to suggest some of the economic as well as political and ecclesiastical functions of the family. In the second chapter I have added some materials about the legal aspects of marriage and divorce. Finally, in the last chapter I have omitted some passages which I now find misleading, and I have added a new discussion of the influence of the marital relationship on Puritan theology.

Most of the new material was written earlier but has not been previously published. An exception is the addition to the last chapter, which appeared as "The Puritan's Marriage with God" in *The South Atlantic Quarterly,* for January, 1949. It is here reprinted with the *Quarterly*'s kind permission.

I retain a lively sense of my debt to those who first helped me

in this undertaking: to my wife, who has been helping me ever
since; to Zoltán Haraszti, whose skill and understanding as an
editor I have come to appreciate more and more; and to the late
Perry Miller, teacher and friend, under whose guidance my study
was begun and whose work will remain a challenge to all who
think about the meaning of New England.

E. S. M.

September 1965

I

Puritanism and Society

*T*HERE was a type of man whom the Puritans never tired of denouncing. He was a good citizen, a man who obeyed the laws, carried out his social obligations, never injured others. The Puritans called him a "civil man," and admitted that he was "outwardly just, temperate, chaste, carefull to follow his worldly businesse, will not hurt so much as his neighbours dog, payes every man his owne, and lives of his owne; no drunkard, adulterer, or quareller; loves to live peaceably and quietly among his neighbours."[1] This man, this paragon of social virtue, the Puritans said, was on his way to Hell, and their preachers continually reminded him of it. Thomas Shepard, for example, addressed him thus:

O, methinks this might pull down men's proud conceits of themselves, especially such as bear up and comfort themselves in their smooth, honest, civil life; such as through education have been washed from all foul sins; they were never tainted with whoredom, swearing, drunkenness, or profaneness; and here they think themselves so safe, that God can not find in his heart to have a thought of damning them.

O, consider of this point, which may make thee pull thine hair from thine head, and turn thy clothes to sackcloth, and run up and down with amazement and paleness in thy face, and horror in thy conscience, and tears in thine eyes. What though thy life be smooth, what though thy outside, thy sepulcher, be painted? O, thou art full

[1] Thomas Hooker, *The Christians Two chiefe Lessons* (London, 1640), p. 213.

1

of rottenness, of sin, within. Guilty, not before men, as the sins of thy life make thee, but before God, of all the sins that swarm and roar in the whole world at this day, for God looks to the heart; guilty thou art therefore of heart whoredom, heart sodomy, heart blasphemy, heart drunkenness, heart buggery, heart oppression, heart idolatry; and these are the sins that terribly provoke the wrath of Almighty God against thee.[2]

Shepard's colleagues said amen. In a thousand sermons they repeated to their congregations that religion was not morality, that righteousness in society was not righteousness before God, that salvation, not civilization, was the chief goal of man, and that salvation was unattainable by good behavior. Only faith in Christ could bring redemption from the sin of Adam, and faith was the free gift of God, not to be won by human efforts. "Not man, but God alone is the author of Regeneration," they insisted, "so men are altogether *passive* in their *Conversion,* and the Eternal Spirit is the only principal Agent therein."[3]

The Puritans believed what they said, believed it passionately, and yet they not only endeavored themselves to live a "smooth, honest, civil life," but tried to force everyone within their power to do likewise. They did not differ from their contemporaries in their views about the importance of salvation as much as they did in their views about behavior. They quarrelled with the Stuart monarchs about such things as playing games on the Sabbath and with Anglican churchmen about vestments and ceremonies. They wrote hundreds of books explaining the exact conduct demanded by God in every human situation. They had, in fact, complete blueprints for a smooth, honest, civil life in family, church, and state, and they were willing to live in the wilderness in order to build a society according to those blueprints. "This was *New-Englands* glory and design," said James Allen in 1679. "They came not hither to assert the prophetical or Priestly office of Christ so much, that were so

[2] Thomas Shepard, *Works,* ed. John Albro (Boston, 1853), I, 29.

[3] Increase Mather, *Some Important Truths Concerning Conversion* (Boston, 1684), pp. 4–5.

fully owned in *Old England,* but his kingly, to bear witness to those truths concerning his visible Kingdome."[4] In other words, the Puritans came to New England not merely to save their souls but to establish a "visible" kingdom of God, a society where outward conduct would be according to God's laws, a society where a smooth, honest, civil life would prevail in family, church, and state.

How can we explain this paradox? How can we reconcile the Puritans' evident concern for social virtues with their professed contempt for them? Why did they pay such homage to good conduct in their social life when it could bring them no nearer to their ultimate goal of salvation? In order to understand Puritan society, including the family, we must first discover the connection between salvation and society. The question divides itself in two: first, why did the Puritans wish to be socially virtuous themselves; and second, why did they wish to force social virtue on others?

Sanctification

The Puritans answered the first question by the enigmatic statement that "sanctification follows justification." Translated into less technical terms, this meant that good social conduct was the result of salvation rather than the cause of it. Before the fall of Adam the reverse had been true. God had made a "covenant of works" with Adam, a covenant according to which God promised salvation in return for perfect obedience to His laws. When Adam disobeyed the laws, he destroyed the covenant and brought corruption on all his descendants. Fallen man, incapable of perfect obedience, was doomed to eternal damnation until God, out of mere mercy, offered him a "covenant of grace." In this covenant God promised salvation not for obedience, since that was now impossible, but for faith (however, a sincere attempt at obedience would necessarily always follow faith). God himself performed both parts of his new covenant: He provided not only salvation but also the faith for which salvation was the reward. Faith was not attainable by mere human volition. It was a belief inspired by the Almighty in those whom He

---

[4] James Allen, *New England's Choicest Blessing* (Boston, 1679), p. 11.

wished to save. And with it came sanctification, a gradual restoration of the faculty for obedience. As long as a man remained on earth, the restoration must be incomplete, but as soon as it began, the man would demonstrate the fact in his outward behavior. He would, so far as possible, love his neighbors and endeavor to obey the laws of God. He would be, in Puritan terms, a "visible saint."

Outwardly this visible saint did not look any different from the "civil man." Both exhibited an external obedience to the laws of God that was almost perfect. The difference between them lay in motive. The civil man did the right deeds for the wrong reasons: he was obedient because of education and social restraints. The sanctified man was obedient because the Holy Spirit had disposed him to be so. Cotton Mather could have applied to all good Puritans what he said of his father:

A Noble Demonstration did he give, That they who do *Good Works* BECAUSE they are already *Justified,* will not come short of those who do *Good Works* THAT THEY MAY be *Justified;* and, That they who Renounce all Pretence to *Merit* by their *Good Works,* will more abound in *Good Works* than the greatest *Merit-Mongers* in the World.[5]

The meritmongers, of course, were the Catholics, who believed that good works had merit in themselves and might lead to salvation. The Puritans, denying any merit to the deeds themselves, merely asserted that good works were "the naturall and necisary Companions of the faith which leads to salvation."[6]

Good works, then, however ineffectual to procure salvation, could be evidence of the faith that did procure it. And the desire to see this evidence in their conduct was with the Puritans night and day, driving them to ever greater moral exertions. Of course a "civil" life was no infallible sign of salvation, since it could be produced by external restraints as well as by faith, but an uncivil life was a sure

[5] Cotton Mather, *Parentator* (Boston, 1724), p. 185.

[6] Boston Sermons 1671–1679, manuscript, Massachusetts Historical Society. (Hereafter, Boston Sermons. The manuscript consists of six volumes of notes taken by John Hull of sermons he attended. Since there is no pagination in any of the volumes, particular sermons are designated by date.) Aug. 5, 1677.

sign of damnation. "If you are heedless of your works," the Puritan ministers warned their congregations, "if you will live at randome according to your hearts desire you may be sure you are no believer."[7] No Puritan wanted to be sure that he was "no believer." Consequently every Puritan did his best to obey the laws of God, to be a good citizen, and thus perhaps to bolster faith by concrete evidence of its existence. Take for example this passage from the diary of a godly young man, written during an illness shortly before his death:

After this, many other Comfortable *Evidences* came to my mind; as, The Certainty that there was a Change in me from what I had been; my *Love to the Brethren,* so that if I had only heard of a man Eminently Good, I had immediately a Love to him, tho' I never saw him. Another Evidence, and all that my weak Hand is now able to Write, is, I am sure *Sin* is a *Burden* to me, and God has promised *Rest* unto such, if they come unto Him.

It is uncertain, How Long I may Ly Languishing by this Illness: therefore I was willing to Write something to Comfort me, by Looking on it. The Lord Write the rest in my Heart![8]

The fact that many Puritans kept diaries of this kind helps to explain their pursuit of social virtue: diaries were the reckoning books in which they checked the assets and liabilities of their souls in faith. When they opened these books, they set down lapses of morality with appropriate expressions of repentance and balanced them against the evidences of faith. Cotton Mather made a point of having at least one good action to set down in his diary on every day of the week.[9] The Puritans' strength lay not in confidence but in lack of it: the very necessity of proving their faith to themselves was behind their assurance in presence of peril or profanity. They felt obliged to be civil in order to convince themselves that they were sanctified.

The same reasons that prompted their own good behavior also

[7] Ibid., Aug. 19, 1677.

[8] Cotton Mather, *Early Religion Urged* (Boston, 1694), p. 95.

[9] Cotton Mather, "Diary", Massachusetts Historical Society *Collections*, seventh series, vols. VII and VIII (hereafter "Diary," I or II). See esp. II, 41.

help to explain why the Puritans enforced good behavior on others. "Dost thou keep Gods commandments as thy way, thy jewels, the apple of thy eye, thy life?" John Cotton asked his listeners; "and dost thou desire to bring all thy children and family to the like conscionable obedience, that all thy family may be Gods friends? This is an argument of thy unfained love to God."[10] Similarly Thomas Hooker explained that "the true convert" seeks to destroy all sin: "What ever sins come within his reach, he labors the removal of them, out of the familyes where he dwells, out of the plantations where he lives, out of the companies and occasions, with whom he hath occasion to meet and meddle at any time."[11] Thus a zealous enforcement of morality on others was another way of proving to yourself that you might have faith.

The Covenant

It is easy to understand that personal morality might serve as a test of faith, for faith entailed sanctification, and sanctification entailed morality. But why did the Puritans regard a concern for the morality of others as a sign of faith? The answer lies in the terms of the covenant of grace. That covenant had been made originally with Abraham, and in applying it to themselves the Puritans retained all its original provisions. Said Thomas Shepard: "One and the same covenant, which was made to Abraham in the Old Testament, is for substance the same with that in the New; and this under the New Testament, the very same with that of Abraham's under the Old."[12]

Now Abraham's covenant included not only himself but his "seed" as well. Nor was this word used in a purely figurative sense. It meant his physical descendants, his children, grandchildren, and great-grandchildren, and it meant his immediate household too.

---

[10] John Cotton, *A Practical Commentary, or An Exposition with Observations, Reasons and Uses upon the First Epistle Generall of John* (London, 1656), p. 352.

[11] Thomas Hooker, *The Application of Redemption* (London, 1659), p. 684.

[12] Shepard, *Works*, III, 521.

Therefore when he promised faith and the sanctified life that faith was supposed to bring, he promised not only for himself but for his whole family, and he was obliged to do all he could to make them fulfill the promise. A Christian in adopting Abraham's covenant undertook the same obligations. "If God make a Covenant, to be a God to thee and thine," John Cotton pointed out, "then it is thy part to see it, that thy children and servants be Gods people."[13] Cotton extended the obligation even further by adding, in another book, that "when we undertake to be obedient to him [God]," we undertake not only "in our owne names, and for our owne parts, but in the behalfe of every soule that belongs to us . . . our wives, and children, and servants, and kindred, and acquaintance, and all that are under our reach, either by way of subordination, or co-ordination."[14] Similarly Thomas Shepard, in urging the duties of Sabbath observance, called upon the heads of families to see to the obedience of the whole household:

. . . our children, servants, strangers who are within our gates, are apt to profane the Sabbath; we are therefore to improve our power over them for God, in restraining them from sin, and in constraining them (as far as we can) to the holy observance of the rest of the Sabbath, lest God impute their sins to us, who had power (as Eli in the like case) to restrain them and did not; and so our families and consciences be stained with their guilt and blood.[15]

The quotations suggest that though the covenant of grace was made with an individual believer, the promises he made were undertaken not just for himself but in behalf of his whole household. All the members of his family were expected to exhibit sanctified or at least civil behavior, and he must see to it that they did so. This duty to enforce good behavior in the family was the germ of all political and ecclesiastical authority. Since Abraham's covenant had included *all* his descendants, it became eventually the foundation of

[13] John Cotton, *The Way of Life* (London, 1641), p. 91.
[14] John Cotton, *Christ the Fountaine of Life* (London, 1651), pp 33–34.
[15] Shepard, *Works*, III, 263.

God's dealings with the whole tribe of Israel. Christians had inherited the covenant in all three forms, not only as individuals and as
families, but as successors to the tribe of Israel too. As Zwingli put
it: "The same covenant which he [God] entered into with Israel he
has in these latter days entered into with us, that we may be one
people with them, one church and may have also one covenant. . . .
Christian people are now that elect race which the Hebrews once
were . . . a people sought and obtained by the blood of Christ."[16]
Protestants who followed Zwingli or Calvin, including the Puritans,
accepted this idea[17] and formulated their political and ecclesiastical
theory upon it. Though they made no attempt to establish a tribe of
Christians, they regarded every Christian state and every Christian
church as a successor to the tribe of Israel. All the members of such
bodies, they thought, were bound by covenant to God.

Here another contradiction begins to become apparent. It is well
known that Puritans and other Calvinists thought that the number
of God's elect was comparatively few in any body of men. Every
state, every church, even every family must contain some who were
destined for damnation. The Puritans did their best to exclude all
but visible saints from their churches, but they had to confess that
it was impossible to keep out hypocritical civil men. A hypocrite
might give such an appearance of sanctification as to deceive the
very angels.[18] He might even deceive himself.[19] Similarly there

[16] Samuel M. Jackson, ed., *Selected Works of Huldreich Zwingli* (Philadel-
phia, 1901), pp. 227, 233.
[17] See Gottlob Schrenk, *Gottesreich und Bund im alteren Protestantismus*
(Gütersloh, 1923), and Perry Miller, *The New England Mind: The Seventeenth Century* (New York, 1939), pp. 365–491.
[18] John Cotton, *The Covenant of Grace: Discovering The Great Work of a
Sinners Reconciliation to God* (London, 1655) pp. 58–80.
[19] "How farr may a hipocrite goe? Ans. he may doe much and reach high
have great illumination to understand and teach others.
2ly he may have Powerfull Convictions, and make clear Confessions of sinn
with much agravation
3ly he may be under awakening and fear; to reject temptations to be afraid
of sin
4ly he may be terrified under aprehension of sin when comitted because of
wrath to Come many mens Consciences Come after this to be seared and thinke
they are saffe.

were "some unbelievers in every family."[20] "In the Church and Congregation," John Cotton explained, "you shall find some wheat, some chaffe, some good corn, some tares; so in the best families; you shall finde a mixture of good and bad together."[21]

How, then, could the covenant of grace, which dealt with salvation, include a whole family, a whole church, or a whole state? The Puritans never gave a completely satisfactory answer to this question, but they did give an answer. The covenant, they said, when applied to a group, originated in, but was not the same as, the covenant of an individual. It had different terms and a different name. It was called a family covenant or a church covenant or a state covenant, instead of a covenant of grace, and the group engaging in it promised external obedience instead of faith and received external, temporal prosperity instead of eternal salvation. Since every group contained unbelievers, no group as such was capable of salvation. God's covenant with a family, a church, or a state, therefore, as well as his covenant with the tribe of Israel, concerned this world, not the next. You cannot obey me in heart and in spirit, He told the members of these bodies, but you can at least do me honor

---

5ly he may have Earnest longings after the state of the blessed, take Paines, think well speake well of the People of god. desire to be joyned with them in his death. many desire to be happy that take no care to be holy.

6ly he may repent of his sin, confess sin, and outwardly foresake sin, weep Put on sacloth go softly

7ly he may be a temporary believer in Jesus Christ trust in him, wait on him, hope to be saved by him. he may be ravished, delighted, with the Privileges of saints. he may be carefull in all externall duties.

8ly he may pray in his affliction and god may Answer and deliver.

9ly he may be eminent and zealous in Profession and wittness to the trouth look like one of the worthies of the Camp of Israel.

10ly he may enjoy all the Privileges of the gospell and outwardly Proffit also by them.

11thly he may bring much glory to god and doe good to many souls

12ly he may have, enjoy, keep his hopes tell he dyeth and Comes into the other world.

Where as many Poor believers meet with much Cross wind and weather. here is a great deal and all may be without saving grace. . . ." (Boston Sermons, April 6, 1679, Samuel Willard)

[20] John Cotton, *The Covenant of Gods free Grace* (London, 1645), p. 6.
[21] *Ibid.*, p. 7.

by not breaking my laws openly and publicly; if you as a people will perform outward obedience to my commands, I will give you outward prosperity as a people. On the other hand, if you disobey me outwardly, I will destroy you as utterly as I destroyed Sodom and Gomorrha.[22]

Thus appears another motive for enforcing a smooth, honest, civil life. Zeal for the morality of others was not only a sign of salvation; it was also a practical means of enjoying outward prosperity. Quite apart from his individual relationship to God through the covenant of grace, every Christian participated in a social relationship to him through a social covenant. The Christian's family, church, and state had each promised to give outward obedience to God in every respect. Consequently every Christian was bound to obey God not merely as a sanctified man (in order to prove to himself that he was saved) but as a member of each group to which he belonged. If he failed, he not only demonstrated his own damnation, but he brought the temporal wrath of God upon his family, upon his church, and upon his state.

In New England these ideas penetrated to every level of society. In 1656 one miserable girl, significantly named "Tryal Pore," who had committed the sin of fornication, confessed to the Middlesex County Court that "by this my sinn I have not only donn what I can to Poull doune Jugmente from the lord on my selve but allso apon the place where I live."[23] In view of such a belief the reason for restraining and punishing sin is obvious. Since the whole group had promised obedience to God, the whole group would suffer for the sins of any delinquent member, unless that member were punished. By publicly punishing him the group testified to their disapproval of his actions and so escaped responsibility for them. Incessant vigilance, however, was essential in order to prevent any sin from going unpunished. It was as if a district occupied by a

---

[22] Cf. Perry Miller, *The New England Mind; The Seventeenth Century*, pp. 365–401.

[23] Manuscript files of Middlesex, Massachusetts, County Court (hereafter Middlesex Files), folder 28, group 5.

military force were given notice that for any disorder the whole community would be penalized, innocent and guilty alike. Every Christian state, church, and family had received such a notice from God. Its effect upon the godly members of such bodies was an extraordinary zeal for enforcement of the laws of God.

The laws of God, as the Puritans understood them, covered all human actions. In order, therefore, to live either a civil or a sanctified life and in order to induce such a life in others, it was necessary to be thoroughly familiar with the laws. To Adam in his original innocence such a familiarity was no problem, for he possessed it by nature. The laws had been written in his heart and mind by the finger of God, and he obeyed them instinctively. The fall, however, had destroyed his good instinct, darkened his heart, and dimmed his reason, so that his posterity could perceive but faintly what had been clear to him. When fallen man tried unaided to discern the laws of God, corruption cast a mist before his vision. Though he could perceive enough of the precepts to justify his damnation for disobedience of them, he could not perceive enough to know the right action for every occasion. Even the Greek and Roman philosophers, who went as far as unassisted human reason could hope to go, had never truly found the good life. Christians, on the other hand, had been given a priceless gift, by which the partial loss of their rational faculties was compensated—the Scriptures. Here God had set down his laws in black and white, and here every man could read them and learn how to act in every circumstance. Even those who ran could read the laws in the Ten Commandments, where the whole had been summarized in simple imperatives.[24]

The Puritans made no attempt to read while they ran. They studied minutely every phrase of the Scriptures and extracted from it the last ounce of meaning, so that each one of the Ten Commandments meant volumes of prohibitions and injunctions to them. Apart from the first one, the commandment which carried the

---

[24] ". . . all the sins and good things found in the whole Bible, are to be ranked within the Compasse of the ten Commandments" (John Cotton, *Practical Commentary upon John*, p. 235).

greatest weight of meaning was probably the fifth: "Honour thy
father and thy mother: that thy days may be long upon the land."
This command summarized all of God's laws concerning the organization of society, not only his laws about family organization, but
his laws about political and ecclesiastical organization as well.

But if the rules were all encompassed in the fifth commandment,
it required no little skill in theology to derive them from it. When
Puritan ministers undertook to explain human relations, whether
in family, church, or state, they relied not simply on the injunctions
of scripture but on a series of highly developed and widely accepted
concepts, which we may call the order of creation, the social order,
the logic of relationships, and the origin of relationships.

The order of creation

Puritan ministers were fond of saying that God was a God of order,
and they were prepared to support the affirmation by metaphysics.
They were as ready as the Scholastic theologians to juggle with
being and essence and substance, with constant and inconstant
natures, with elements and elementaries.[25] But since they directed
their words to plain people and prided themselves on a "plain
style,"[26] they usually spared their listeners the intricacies of the
metaphysical dialect. When the order of the universe had been dis-
tilled into a Sunday sermon, it came out in a relatively simple and
intelligible form, closely integrated with the whole religious pattern
of sin and redemption.

According to the standard account, God created the world to
express his own glory. Consequently his glory stood as the ultimate
end or purpose of all "beings" animate or inanimate. Every rock,
every cloud, every blade of grass, every beast, man, angel, even
every devil was created to serve God and carry out his will. But all
these "creatures" were not the same, neither in substance nor in
form, nor yet quite the same in purpose. All existed to serve God,

---

[25] See William Ames, *The Marrow of Sacred Divinity* (London, 1643), pp.
1–39; Samuel Willard, *A Compleat Body of Divinity* (Boston, 1736), pp.
111ff.
[26] Perry Miller, *The New England Mind*, ch. xii. "The Plain Style."

but each served him in a different way. Since God was the God of order, he had not created the world upon a principle of equality; for such a procedure would have produced only "an heap of confusion," a world without variety, resembling the monotony of sands on the beach or drops of water in the ocean.[27] Instead he had arranged for every creature but one to serve him indirectly, by serving another creature. With one exception everything in the world had a double purpose: its ultimate end was to serve God, its immediate end to serve another being. And that other being, of course, was man, the chief beneficiary next to God in the scheme of creation. "Though all things were made ultimately for the Glory of God; yet in the Order of their Being, there was a Subordination of them, and they were to serve God, in serving of Man."[28] "This *World* and the things of it, were made for the service and accomodation of man in his way of serving God."[29]

By the command of God man had been made master of the whole visible creation. And as if this were not a sufficient privilege, he had been given the further advantage of "having nothing better than himself, between him and God."[30] While other creatures looked toward God through man, man looked directly at God as both his immediate and his ultimate end.

There was no other sort of Being made after him, to shew, that he was made for no other Created Being. The Creature is to look forward; and there was nothing stood between Man and God, to give him to understand, that nothing should intercept his Heart, but that he ought to make God his immediate End. . . .[31]

[27] William Hubbard, *The Happiness of a People in the Wisdome of their Rulers* (Boston, 1676), p. 8.

[28] Willard, *Compleat Body of Divinity*, p. 124.

[29] Urian Oakes, *A Seasonable Discourse wherein Sincerity and Delight in the Service of God is earnestly pressed upon Professors of Religion* (Cambridge, 1682), p. 27.

[30] Shepard, *Works*, III, 25.

[31] Willard, *Compleat Body of Divinity*, p. 124. Cf. Shepard, *Works*, III, 25: "For although all inferior creatures are made lastly for God, yet they are made nextly for man; but man, having nothing better than himself, between him and God, is therefore made both lastly and nextly for God; and hence it is that no inferior creature, which comes out and issueth from God, hath such a

Such was the order of the universe as God created it. Clearly no being in it enjoyed better opportunities for advancing the glory of God than did man. His direct connection with God constantly reminded him of his duty, and the whole creation stood by to assist him in it. Yet he failed—and his failure turned the divine order topsy-turvy. When Adam disobeyed God, he made something less than God his end. Instead of acting as the end of the other creatures, he used them as his own end.

Man had originally an Empire and Dominion over these creatures here below. . . .

But sin hath inverted this Order, and brought confusion upon earth. Man is dethroned, and become a servant and slave to those things that were made to serve him, and he puts those things in his heart, that God hath put under his feet.[32]

Sin, in other words, was disorder, a substitution of God's creations for God himself as the end of man. As Samuel Willard told the Old South Church: "The nature of sin is a changing of the object," for "man by sin is gone from god and fallen upon the creature."[33] Since the sin of Adam was inherited by his posterity, the whole world was confronted with confusion. Man occupied the key position in the order that God had ordained, and when man neglected his end, the rest of creation likewise lost its purpose. For if man failed to serve God, the other creatures could no longer "serve God, in serving of Man"; they were deprived of their immediate end and so of their connection with the ultimate end. "Man was the mean betwixt God and the Creature to convey all good with all the constancy of it, and therefore when Man breaks, Heaven and Earth breaks all asunder, the Conduit being cracked and displaced there can be no conveyance from the Fountain."[34] Hence the creatures since the

reflux and return again back unto God, as man hath; because, in and by this reflux and return into him, man's mortal being is eternally preserved, like water running into the sea again, from whence it first came."
[32] Urian Oakes, *A Seasonable Discourse*, p. 27.
[33] *Boston Sermons*, July 6, 1679.
[34] Thomas Hooker, *The Application of Redemption*, p. 59.

fall of Adam existed in vain as far as their original purpose was concerned and served only as tools for the lusts of degenerate men. Not that their vanity was deliberate; in fact, "the whole Creation groaneth to be delivered from its subjection to vanity."[35] But as long as sin remained, so long would disorder remain, and so long would the creatures exist in vain.

For this miserable condition of the world Christ had brought the remedy, and at the last day he would completely restore order to the world. In the meantime his remedy brought relief wherever it was adopted. The believer who was justified by faith in Christ was freed from the effects of sin and so from disorder; the operation of grace in his heart directed him to his proper end. "If sin be (as it is) an aversion or turning away of the soul from God to something else besides him . . . then in the work of grace there is a conversion and turning of the soul towards God again, as to the best and cheifest good of all."[36] Sin was a violation of order, grace a restoration of order. All the main tenets of Christian religion could be stated in terms of this concept, and the Puritans so stated them again and again. In almost every sermon the ministers found occasion to warn their listeners that "the onely sutable adequate ultimate object of the soul of man is god himselfe,"[37] that "all true christians have Christ as the scope and End of their lives,"[38] that "a christian may and ought to desire many things as meanes, but God alone, as his End, as his last end,"[39] that "all things but the

---

[35] This was the doctrine of a sermon preached by Thomas Thatcher, Boston Sermons, May 12, 1678.

[36] Richard Mather, *Farewell Exhortation* (Cambridge, 1657), p. 20. Cf. Thomas Hooker, *Application of Redemption*, p. 673: ". . . there must be an Aversion and turning from the Creature, before there can be a conversion unto God; he came from God to the Creature, he must return from the Creature to God: but his aversion is first, that is, from his abusive cleaving to the Creature; for in truth, sin is nothing else but an inordinate affecting of these inferior things. . . ."

[37] Boston Sermons, July 6, 1679.

[38] Ibid., July 6, 1672.

[39] Jonathan Mitchell, manuscript, "Sermons from Psalms," p. 65a. Massachusetts Historical Society.

last end, are no further good then as they lead to him,"[40] that "no Creature, that is finite, can be the end of the Soul, nor give satisfaction to it."[41]

The attitude toward the world expressed in these statements was not hostile. Contrary to popular impression the Puritan was no ascetic. If he continually warned against the vanity of the creatures as misused by fallen man, he never praised hair shirts or dry crusts. He liked good food, good drink, and homely comforts; and while he laughed at mosquitoes, he found it a real hardship to drink water when the beer gave out. In using the good things of this world, however, he kept in mind the order which God had ordained; he sought God's glory in "eating and drinking, sleeping and recreating."[42] If it was a question of a good bed, he knew that "the end of all Sleep and Rest, is to refresh the Spirit and strengthen the body, and help digestion" and that "therefore so much Sleep as may help digestion and comfort and refresh a mans body and spirit, God allows," but that if a man grows "to love Sleep and Ease . . . and never looks how to imploy it to Gods service, now hee propounds no right end." If he felt the need of recreation, he knew that God did not forbid innocent play; but he took care even in sport to attend the order of God, for he knew that pastime was disorderly and unlawful when "wee look at no higher end than our own pleasure." When he was hungry, he did not hesitate to satisfy his appetite with good meat and drink, but he made the service of God his end in so doing. He strengthened his body with food in order to serve God with greater vigor. For he knew that "we may chear our bodies, but we must not terminate all this in eating and drinking, for then it is a lust of the flesh."[43]

The incidence of such ideas in the daily life of a good Puritan is indicated by John Winthrop's account of how he came to understand them:

[40] John Cotton, *Briefe Exposition upon Ecclesiastes*, p. 29.
[41] Thomas Hooker, *A Comment upon Christ's Last Prayer* (London, 1650), p. 525.
[42] From the copy of a sermon by Thomas Leadbeater in the Commonplace Book of Edward Taylor, Massachusetts Historical Society.
[43] John Cotton, *Practical Commentary upon John*, pp. 125–128.

When I had some tyme abstained from suche worldly delights
as my heart most desired, I grewe very melancholick and uncom-
fortable, for I had been more careful to refraine from an outward
conversation in the world, then to keepe the love of the world out
of my heart, or to uphold my conversation in heaven; which caused
that my comfort in God failinge, and I not daringe to meddle with
any earthly delights, I grewe into a great dullnesse and discontent:
which beinge at last perceived, I examined my heart, and findinge
it needfull to recreate my minde with some outward recreation, I
yielded unto it, and by a moderate exercise herein was much re-
freshed; but heere grewe the mischiefe: I perceivinge that God
and mine owne conscience did alowe me so to doe in my need, I
afterwards tooke occasion, from the benefite of Christian libertie,
to pretend need of recreation when there was none, and so by degrees I ensnared my heart so farre in worldly delights, as I cooled
the graces of the spirit by them: Whereby I perceive that in all
outward comforts, althoughe God allowe us the use of the things
themselves, yet it must be in sobriety, and our hearts must be kept
free, for he is jealous of our love, and will not endure any pretences
in it.[44]

The Social Order

The world was created for man, but man was created for God.
Such was the order of creation. What, then, was the order of
society? From what has been said it appears that men in relation
to God and to the other creatures were equal. It did not follow,
however, that men were equal among themselves. Since God had
created the world with some beings subordinate to others, he
naturally proceeded upon the same principle in constructing human
society. Subordination was indeed the very soul of order, and
the Almighty as a God of order formed his earthly kingdom in a
pattern of subordination. *"Order,"* said John Norton, *"is a divine
disposal, of superior and inferior relations, in humane or Christian
societies."*[45] "Nothing therefore can be imagined," added William
Hubbard, "more remote either from right reason, or true religion,

---

[44] *Winthrop Papers* (Boston: The Massachusetts Historical Society, 1929–), I,
201–202.

[45] John Norton, *Heart of N—England Rent* (Cambridge, 1659), p. 30.

then to think that because we were all once equal at our birth, and shall be again at our death, therefore we should be so in the whole course of our lives."[46] According to Hubbard it was not

the result of time or chance, that some are mounted on horseback, while others are left to travell on foot. That some have with the Centurion power to command, while others are required to obey, *the poor and the rich meet together, the Lord is the maker of them both.* The Almighty hath appointed her that sits behind the mill, *as well as him that ruleth on the throne.*[47]

Such views enjoyed as much popularity in New England as they have in most societies. The Puritans were no levelers. Social classes and the various offices, orders, and positions of social rank existed for them as part of a divinely ordered plan, "so that it appears, whoever is for a parity in any Society, will in the issue reduce things into an heap of confusion."[48] In every Puritan society, therefore, including the family, we may expect to find human relationships clothed in a pattern of superiority and inferiority.

The Puritans indeed honored every kind of superiority among men as part of the divine order: old men were superior to young, educated to uneducated, rich to poor, craftsmen to common laborers, highborn to lowborn, clever to stupid. These differences in age, wealth, birth, and talents, however, did not constitute the order of any particular social group. They were differences similar to the differences between inferior creatures, say between a horse and a dog, differences which merely added richness and complexity to the social order. The order which God had constituted in society presupposed his "appoyntment of mankind to live in Societies, first, of Family, Secondly Church, Thirdly, Common-wealth."[49] For each of these groups He had established a special order, consisting of the relationships which the members were supposed to bear to one another; and respect for this order was the first thing that He

---

[46] William Hubbard, *The Happiness of a People*, p. 10.
[47] Ibid., p. 9.
[48] Ibid., p. 8.
[49] John Cotton, *A Briefe Exposition with Practicall Observations upon the Whole Book of Ecclesiastes* (London, 1654), p. 81.

demanded in all societies, whether of family, church, or state. "Order is the Soul of Common Wealths and Societyes," said one minister.[50] "It is the forme of societies," said another, and he added, "Formes are essential without which things cannot be."[51] "Be lovers of order," urged a third; "learn to know it that you may love it."[52] And they all taught their congregations that "whatever is done against the order that God has constituted is done against God."[53]

The essence of the social order lay in the superiority of husband over wife, parents over children, and master over servants in the family, ministers and elders over congregation in the church, rulers over subjects in the state. A child might possess superior talents and ability to his father, but within the family his father remained superior. A church member might be the richest man in the community, but his pastor held authority over him in the church. In each relationship God had ordained that one party be superior, the other inferior; for when he said, "Honor thy father and thy mother," he meant spiritual and political as well as natural fathers and mothers. Puritan children, studying the famous cathechism prepared by John Cotton, learned to answer the question *"Who are here* [in the fifth commandment] *meant by Father and Mother?"* with the words, "All our Superiours, whether in Family, School, Church, and Common-wealth."[54] When the governors of Massachusetts wished to convict Mrs. Hutchinson of sedition, they charged her with breaking the fifth commandment, because she had tried to play the part rather of *"a Husband than a Wife, and a preacher than a Hearer; and a Magistrate than a Subject."*[55]

[50] John Richardson, *The Necessity of a Well-Experienced Souldiery* (Cambridge, 1679), p. 13.
[51] John Norton, *The Heart of N—England Rent*, p. 30.
[52] Boston Sermons, Jan. 14, 1671/2.
[53] Ibid., Feb. 4, 1676/7.
[54] John Cotton, *Spiritual Milk for Boston Babes* (Cambridge, 1656), p. 4.
[55] Charles F. Adams, ed., *Antinomianism in the Colony of Massachusetts Bay* (Boston, 1894) p. 329.

The social order was not far different from the order of creation: as man ruled over the creatures and as God ruled over man, so parents ruled over children and kings over subjects. God himself was called a king, and kings in turn were called gods by the Bible. All persons in authority, whether in family, church, or state, stood in the place of Christ. Servants were exhorted to regard their masters as gods and to serve them as though they were serving God. Wives were instructed that woman was made ultimately for God but immediately for man.[56] "He for God only, she for God in him," says Milton, and so Eve addresses her husband:

> O thou for whom
> And from whom I was formed flesh of thy flesh,
> And without whom am to no end, my guide
> And head![57]

Evidently wives and servants stood to masters and husbands as other creatures stood to man in general. The subordination of men to each other, however, was not the same as the subordination of other creatures to man; for although the creatures had access to God only through their superior, man—all men, inferior or superior, male or female—could pray to Him directly. Furthermore, all men had immortal souls. Unlike the brute creatures they had to live for the eternal future as well as for the temporal present, and in that future the relations of this life would mean nothing. "The things and relations of this life," said Thomas Hooker, "are like prints left in Sand, there is not the least appearance or remembrance of them. The King remembers not his Crown, the Husband the Wife, Father the Child. . . ."[58] The only relationship which endured beyond this life was that between man and his final end, God in Christ. This was "the only Marriage that cannot be dissolved."[59]

---

[56] "Woman is lastly and as *Homo* (or one of mankinde) for God; but nextly and as *Mulier* (in her proper place and sex) for the man, to be an Help to him . . ." (Jonathan Mitchel, *Nehemiah on the Wall in Troublesome Times* [Cambridge, 1671], p. 6)

[57] *Paradise Lost*, Book IV, lines 299, 440–443.

[58] Thomas Hooker, *A Comment upon Christ's Last Prayer*, p. 367.

[59] Increase Mather, *Practical Truths plainly Delivered* (Boston, 1718), p. 56.

Consequently every man must strive in this world to enter into that marriage, a goal which could never be attained if he set too much value upon his human relations. For a child to make too much of its parents, a wife of her husband, a subject of his king was to place the creature before the creator, to reverse the order of creation, to repeat the sin of Adam. All social relations must be maintained with a respect to the order of things, in full recognition of the fact that man "ought to make God his immediate End."[60]

The Logic of Relationships

The terms in which an idea is embodied will frequently influence its content. When the Puritans spoke of "relations" and "relatives," they had in mind a number of logical propositions which defined the use of those words much more closely than a modern reader would suppose. Relatives in this special logical sense constituted "affirmative contraries of which the one exists out of a mutual affection of the other."[61] Anyone confronted with this definition and desiring further explanation might have discovered that relatives were also opposite, disagreeing, simple, primary, and artificial. If he failed to understand this elucidation, he would have been told that he obviously knew nothing about logic and that he had better get a copy of the *Dialectica* of Peter Ramus together with a commentary by Mr. George Downame or Mr. Alexander Richardson.[62] Perry Miller has demonstrated the far-reaching influence of the Ramist logic upon the New England mind. He has shown that the Puritans almost invariably phrased their ideas in terms of that logic.[63] Their ideas about society were no exception. In order therefore to understand the terms in which they conceived all social relationships, it is

[60] Samuel Willard, *Compleat Body of Divinity*, p. 124.

[61] "Relata sunt contraria affirmantia, quorum alterum constat e mutua alterius affectione. . ." (Petrus Ramus, *Dialecticae Libri Duo* [London, 1669], pp. 11–12).

[62] Alexander Richardson, *The Logicians School-Master, or a comment upon Ramus Logick* (London, 1657); George Downame, *Commentarii in P. Rami Dialecticam* (London, 1669); Petrus Ramus, *Dialecticae Libri Duo* (London, 1669.)

[63] See Perry Miller, *The New England Mind*, esp. pp. 111–239.

necessary to have in mind the general structure of the Ramist system and to examine more closely the section of it which pertained to relations.

Ramist logic in the eyes of its followers was not simply a way of reasoning: it was a copy of reality. As one Harvard student put it in 1647, "The art of logic is in the thing."[64] He did not mean that logic was an empirical science but that the "ideas" or "arguments" of Ramist logic, such as "relative," "opposite," and "contrary," had been placed by God in the actual framework of creation and were just as real as a man or a stone or a tree. Ramist logic purported to discover the structure of things, and it affirmed that its "arguments" named the actual rafters and joists and studding of the universe. Ramism, as Miller has pointed out, was Platonic realism revived once again.[65]

The terms, however, which the Ramists used to describe reality, derived from Aristotle rather than Plato. When examined, they appear to be the old categories of the *Organon* elevated to equality with primary substance and arranged in a new pattern. The distinguishing feature of the pattern was its symmetry: reality fell very neatly into dichotomies in a hierarchical order, so that its structure could be diagramed on a single page with the assistance of successively larger brackets.[66] Anyone wishing to discover the nature of a thing and its relationships to other things, whether it was a stone or a color or a cause or a virtue, had only to refer to this diagram, where he could trace its attributes from the special to the general.

Though all the "arguments" in this scheme expressed relationships of things in the general sense, the term "relative" was used only in a much more specific sense. Things might be related in numerous ways, but they were called "relatives" only if they were

---

[64] "Ars logica est in re." Harvard College Theses Logicae 1647, in Samuel E. Morison, *Harvard College in the Seventeenth Century* (Cambridge, 1936), p. 588.

[65] Perry Miller, *The New England Mind*, pp. 177–178.

[66] See diagram reproduced in Miller, *The New England Mind*, p. 126.

related in one particular way.[67] This particular way demanded that they be affirmative contraries related to each other in such a way as to be mutual causes of each other. Breaking down this definition, one finds that "contraries" were opposites of a particular kind, qualified by the clause *quorum unum uni tantum opponitur*.[68] They were "well matched striking downright blows."[69] They were, in other words, exact opposites, opposing each other in a "one to one" relationship (the only other kind of opposites, known as "disparates"; were unequal opposites). Contraries, following the regular pattern of dichotomy, divided into two types: negative contraries expressed an opposition between something and nothing; affirmative contraries between "things in nature, or things *positive*."[70] Affirmative contraries were subdivided finally into the basic arguments of relatives and adverses. The difference between these lay in the total opposition of adverses (heat and cold, virtue and vice) and the partial agreement of relatives (buyer and seller, father and son). Relatives furthermore were the mutual cause and effect of each other, or in the words of our original definition, they existed out of mutual affection of one another. For example, buyer causes seller and seller causes buyer, so that if buyer exists, seller must also exist, or if seller ceases to exist, buyer also ceases. "And because of this mutual cause of relation relatives are said to be at the same time in nature, as whoever perfectly knows the one also knows the other."[71]

This welter of definitions has been brought forward because the Puritans thought of human relationships in these terms. The relations which formed the substance of social order all fell under the classification of relatives (the favorite example of relatives in the

---

[67] "All arguments are not relatives." Harvard College Theses Logicae 1653, in Samuel E. Morison, *Harvard College in the Seventeenth Century*, p. 590.
[68] Petrus Ramus, *Dialecticae Libri Duo*, p. 11.
[69] Alexander Richardson, *The Logicians School-Master*, p. 159.
[70] Ibid., p. 163.
[71] "Et ob hanc mutuam relationis causam relata dicuntur simul esse natura, ut qui alterum perfecte norit, norit et reliquum" (Ramus, *Dialecticae Libri Duo*, p. 12).

textbooks was that of parents and children) and therefore were
governed by the "law of relatives," as the definition which we have
been pursuing was called. Since logic purported only to delineate
and define the structure of reality, the law of relatives was merely
a law of definition, not of conduct. But definition is an ancient in-
strument of argumentation, and the Puritans often used it in their
efforts to subdue New England to the will of God.

Exactly how the law of relatives entered their thinking about
social order can be seen in Thomas Hooker's defense of congregational polity. Hooker confounded Presbyterians and Episcopalians
alike by defining the ground out from under their feet with the
Ramist law of relatives. The following passage contains his proof
of the congregational tenet that a minister is created only by the
election of a congregation, and that therefore ordination is only an
"approbation" of a minister already established.

Argument 1.

Its taken from that *relation,* which God according to the rule of
reason hath placed betwixt the *Pastor* and the *People,* whence the
dispute growes.
*One Relate gives being and the essentiall constituting causes to
the other.*
But Pastor and People, Shepheard and Flocke, are Relates, Ergo.

. . . . . .

The *Proposition* is supported by the *fundamentall* principles of
reason, so that he must rase out the received *rules of Logick* that
must reject it: *Relata sunt, quorum unum constat e mutua alterius
affectione:* and hence all men that will not stifle and stop the passage of rationall discourse, forthwith infer, that therefore they are
simul natura, are together in nature one with another: a *father,*
as a relate or father, is *not before his son,* buying before selling,
selling before buing [*sic*].
Assumption. That *Pastor* and People, Shepherd and *Flock* are
relates, no man that hath sipped on Logick, hath a forehead to
gainsay.
The *premises* being so sure and plain, the *conclusion* must be
certain and undeniable.

And hence also it will follow, that they are *simul natura,* and the one cannot be before the other; *there cannot be a Pastor before there be a People, which choose him. Episcopalis ordinatio sine titulo, est aeque ridicula* (sayes *Ames,* med. Th. 1. I. c. 39. p.35.) *ac siquis maritus fingeretur esse absque uxore.* And indeed it is a ridiculous thing to conceit the contrary.

And hence again it followes, that *Ordination,* which comes after, is *not* for the *constitution* of the Officer, but the *approbation* of him so constituted in his Office. For, *Relata* are *unum uni,* sayes the rule, and compleatly give mutuall causes each to the other.[72]

The same law of relatives that Hooker used in support of congregationalism gave point to John Cotton's rhetorical question condemning democracy. "If the people be governors," he asked, "who shall be governed?"[73] To the modern ear the rhetoric of this question is cheap indeed, but to anyone imbued in the logic of relatives it demonstrated that democracy was no government at all. For governor and governed were relatives, and since relatives were contraries, the same persons could not be both governors and governed: it was palpably impossible that a group of persons should be contrary to themselves. Ramist logic thus provided a club to beat the dogs of democracy and prelacy. The law of relatives, though it offered no directions for conduct, could be used to identify and combat deviations from the social order that God prescribed.

The Origin of Relationships

The God of order who made the creatures subordinate to man had arranged human society into a network of dual relationships (relatives) in which one party was usually subordinate to the other: ruler and subject, husband and wife, parent and child, master and servant. God had provided these forms, and He had created the men to fill them; but as they came from his hands men enjoyed only one social relationship, the natural one which they bore to

[72] Thomas Hooker, *A Survey of the Summe of Church Discipline* (London, 1648), part 2, pp. 67–68.

[73] Thomas Hutchinson, *The History of the Colony and Province of Massachusetts Bay* (Cambridge, Mass., 1936), I, 415.

their parents. The other forms of social relation had to be filled by the voluntary action of individuals.

Amongst such who by no impression of nature, no rule of providence, or appointment from God, or reason, have power each over other, *there must of necessity be a mutuall ingagement,* each of the other by their free consent, before by any rule of God they have any right or power, or can exercise either, each towards the other.[74]

Such voluntary relations originated in a contract or "covenant" between two parties. "All Relations which are neither naturall nor violent, but voluntary, are by vertue of some covenant."[75] Before any two individuals could stand together in any social relation besides that of parent and child or conqueror and captive, they had to covenant with each other, "by their free consent." "A Covenant, in generall, may then be thus described," said Samuel Willard. *"It is a mutual Engagement between two Parties."*[76]

While most social relations originated in a free choice, it did not follow that anyone could choose to remain aloof from those relations. Since God had ordained that men live together in family, church, and state, they must do so. Although Puritans believed that a free consent was essential to a covenant, they also believed that freedom consisted in the opportunity to obey the will of God. The freedom of any individual, therefore, lay only in the choice of what state should govern him, what church he should worship in, and to some extent what family he should live in. When the Puritans were persecuted in one state, they followed the example of the apostle and fled, not to escape from government, but to exchange

---

[74] Thomas Hooker, *Survey of the Summe of Church Discipline,* part 1, p. 69.

[75] Increase Mather, *Renewal of Covenant the great Duty incumbent on decaying or distressed Churches* (Boston, 1677), preface. Cf. John Cotton, *The Way of the Churches of Christ in New-England* (London, 1645), p. 4; John Davenport, *The Power of Congregational Churches Asserted and vindicated* (London, 1672, p. 39; Richard Mather, *An Apologie of the Churches in New-England for Church-Covenant* (London, 1643), pp. 21-22.

[76] Samuel Willard, *Covenant-Keeping the Way to Blessedness* (Boston, 1682), p. 6.

bad government for good. Men who chose to come to New England had to take an oath of allegiance to the government there.[77] Furthermore, since God had ordained that men live in families, the new government required them to do so. The selectmen of every town in Massachusetts had orders to dispose of all single persons "to servise, or otherwise."[78] If a single man could not afford to hire servants and so set up a household or "family" of his own, he was obliged to enter another family, either as a servant or as a boarder, subjecting himself to the domestic government of its head. His only freedom lay in the choice of families, and if he failed to make a choice, the selectmen would make it for him. The government could not, of course, compel a man to become a church member, for that depended upon God's granting him faith, but every citizen was required by law to attend Sunday worship.

Thus the fact that most social relations originated in a "free" consent did not by any means frustrate the scheme of order which God had ordained. It does indicate, however, that that order was not an order of caste. The doctrine of the covenant combined with the law of relatives effectively expressed the fact that no social class was a real entity in itself. The order of society was a relative order consisting of various relationships in which only two parties could participate. "The notion of a Covenant," said Willard, "belongs to the head of Relation, now all Relations are made up of two parties: every Relate must have its correlate. . . ." And no relate could have more than one correlate, so that no more than two parties could partake in a covenant. "For although there may be ten thousand Men engaged in a Covenant (thus all the Subjects in a Kingdom do stand in Covenant-relation to their Prince) yet still they constitute but one party in that engagement."[79]

[77] Max Farrand, ed., *The Laws and Liberties of Massachusetts: Reprinted from the Copy of the 1648 Edition in the Henry E. Huntington Library.* (Cambridge, Mass., 1929) p. 56. (Hereafter *Mass Laws of 1648*).

[78] Nathaniel B. Shurtleff, ed., *The Records of the Governor and Company of the Massachusetts Bay in New England*, 5 vols. (Boston, 1853–1854), I, 186. (Hereafter *Massachusetts Records*).

[79] Willard, *Covenant-Keeping the Way to Blessedness*, pp. 6–7.

Here lies the final significance of the fact that the Puritans conceived social order in terms of dual relationships: no man could be a servant or a minister or a king in any general or absolute sense but only in relation to another man or group of men. In spite of the popular misconception of the power exercised by the New England clergy, Puritanism had no place for a priestly caste. By the law of relatives a minister ceased to be a minister when he lost his congregation, and he lost it if either he or the congregation broke the covenant between them. Hooker reduced the idea of caste to absurdity when he imagined that a man should "come to a servant, and tell him, I am a master of servants. . . . *Therefore thou art my servant, and must do the work of my family.*" Similarly Hooker thought it would be strange "that *a man* should be a *generall Husband* to all women, or a woman a *generall wife* to all men, because *marriage-covenant is common* to all."[80] Although the social mobility of early New England society was not the product of such abstract theories as the doctrine of the covenant and the law of relatives, these theories at least harmonized with the fact of mobility and provided the forms in which it moved.

The order of society, then, consisted in certain dual relationships, most of them originating in agreements between the persons related and all arranged in a pattern of authority and subjection. But how did one relationship differ from another? If all followed the same general pattern, what distinguishing features pertained to each? God, according to the Puritans, had also answered this question: he had assigned special and peculiar duties to each relationship. With the duties which He assigned to rulers and subjects and to pastors and congregations this book is not concerned. It is confined, instead, to the duties of husbands and wives, parents and children, masters and servants, and with the implications of these relationships in the society the Puritans founded in seventeenth-century New England.

[80] Thomas Hooker, *Survey of the Summe of Church Discipline*, part 1, p. 67.

II

Husband
and Wife

WHEN God presented Eve to Adam, he "Solemnized the First Marriage that ever was"[1] and in so doing gave his sanction to marriage itself. Therefore, the Puritans said, with an eye on the Catholics, those who "speak reproachfully of it do both impeach God's Wisdom and Truth."[2] The Puritans refused to regard marriage as a sacrament, but they also abjured the ideal of celibacy as a condition purer and holier than marriage. "God was of another mind" than those who believe in "the Excellency of Virginity," for he had provided the first man with a wife.[3] According to John Cotton:

Women are Creatures without which there is no comfortable Living for man: it is true of them what is wont to be said of Governments, *That bad ones are better than none:* They are a sort of Blasphemers then who dispise and decry them, and call them *a necessary Evil,* for they are *a necessary Good;* such as it was not good that man should be without."[4]

In the "First Marriage that ever was" neither party had had a choice. Adam and Eve were husband and wife as naturally as they were man and woman. Adam's descendants, on the other hand, had

---

[1] Samuel Willard, *A Compleat Body of Divinity* (Boston, 1726), p. 125.
[2] *Loc. cit.*
[3] John Cotton, *A Meet Help: Or, a Wedding Sermon, Preached at New-Castle in New England, June 19, 1694* (Boston, 1699), p. 15.
[4] Cotton, *A Meet Help*, p. 14.

to choose their own mates. Every proper marriage since the first was founded on a covenant to which the free and voluntary consent of both parties was necessary. The difference ended, however, when the mate was chosen. Since time began no man and woman had ever been allowed to fix the terms upon which they would agree to be husband and wife. God had established the rules of marriage when he solemnized the first one, and he had made no changes in them since then. The covenant of marriage was a promise to obey those rules, without conditions and without reservations. "Many other Covenants are bounded by the makers," Samuel Willard admitted, "but all the duties of this covenant is appointed by God."[5] Therefore "When husband and wife neglect their duties they not only wrong each other, but they provoke God by breaking his law."[6]

Whether bride and groom recited the terms of their covenant in detail at the wedding is not clear. So far as I am aware, no written copy of a seventeenth-century New England marriage covenant exists. The promises were made orally then as they are now, and although the Puritans insisted upon a public record of every marriage, they never recorded the covenant itself but simply the fact of its having been made. However, even if the words had been preserved, the chances are that they would not reveal much; in all likelihood they simply stated the promise of each person to take the other as husband or wife. The duties of the relationship were probably hidden behind the terms "husband" and "wife", which automatically implied to the Puritans, as they do to us, certain unmistakable rights and duties. But if the actual words remain a mystery, the rest of the procedure is clear; and it sheds some light on the relationship of husband and wife.

When the Puritans left England, several steps were necessary to the proper accomplishment of a marriage in that country: (1) espousals *per verba de futuro,* or a contract to marry made in the future tense, corresponding to a modern engagement but more

---

[5] Boston Sermons, Sept. 30, 1672.
[6] Benjamin Wadsworth, *The Well-Ordered Family* (Boston, 1712) p. 40.

binding; (2) publication of the banns, or announcement that this contract *de futuro* had been made; (3) execution of the espousal contract by a contract of marriage in the present tense, *per verba de praesenti,* solemnized at church and followed by a special service; (4) a celebration of the event with feasting and gaiety at the home of the groom; (5) sexual intercourse. The penalty for not following all the above steps was slight. English marriage throughout the seventeenth century remained under the control of the Church of England, and since that church left the Catholic fold before the Council of Trent had revised the law of marriage, the English law retained all the confusion that had characterized the canon law during the Middle Ages. Like the medieval church, the Anglican recognized as valid all marriages that had been consummated in sexual union and preceded by a contract, either public or private, with witnesses or without, in the present tense or the future tense. Neglect of any of the steps listed above was discouraged by spiritual penalties but not punished by any civil court. The result was an abundance of bigamous and clandestine marriages.[7]

In England the conservatism of the Anglican church prevented the passage of laws which would have ended clandestine marriage. In New England, far from episcopal interference, the Puritans were able to regularize all proceedings so as to leave no doubt about the existence and validity of every marriage. According to the Puritan system, no couple could join themselves in marriage before publishing their intention to do so by an announcement made at three successive public meetings, or by a written notice attached to the meetinghouse door for fourteen days. The wedding itself took place under supervision of the state. Although marriage retained a solemn religious significance, all ecclesiastical ceremonies connected with it were abandoned; and the minister was replaced by a civil magistrate, who was forbidden to join any couple unless they had

[7] This paragraph is based on Chilton L. Powell, "Marriage in Early New England," *New England Quarterly,* I, 323–334, on the same author's *English Domestic Relations 1487–1653* (New York, 1917), and on George E. Howard, *A History of Matrimonial Institutions* (Chicago and London, 1904), I, 253–364.

been "published" according to law. Within a month after the ceremony the bridegroom was required to report the marriage to the town clerk under penalty of a fine.[8]

Civil magistrates continued to perform all marriages in New England until 1686.[9] At that time, when charters had been revoked and royal government established throughout New England, ministers were also empowered to perform the ceremony, but it gained no added religious significance by this innovation. In other respects the procedure remained the same, and although the change may have irritated New Englanders, it never constituted a serious grievance. Even Samuel Sewall, who would not attend a wedding of cousins because of the Mosaic prohibition,[10] never refused a wedding invitation because a minister was to preside. In 1719 he himself was married by the Reverend Joseph Sewall, his own son.[11] Ministers themselves made no great objection to performing marriages, and when charter government was restored, the innovation was retained.

The ease with which the change was brought about is perhaps explained by the fact that throughout the seventeenth century ministers frequently presided at formal espousal ceremonies and took the occasion to preach "espousal sermons."[12] The only colony

[8] William H. Whitmore, ed., *The Colonial Laws of Massachusetts: Reprinted from the edition of 1672* (Boston, 1890; hereafter *Massachusetts Laws of 1672*), pp. 101, 102, 130; David Pulsifer, ed., *Records of the Colony of New Plymouth in New England*, 12 vols. (Boston, 1855–61; hereafter *Plymouth Records*), XI, 190; Charles J. Hoadly, ed., *Records of the Colony or Jurisdiction of New Haven* (Hartford, 1858; hereafter *New Haven Records*), pp. 599–600; J. H. Trumbull et al., eds., *Public Records of the Colony of Connecticut*, 15 vols. (Hartford, 1850–90; hereafter *Connecticut Records*), I, 47–48, 105–106.

[9] Howard, *Matrimonial Institutions*, II, 137; Powell, "Marriage in Early New England," *New England Quarterly*, I, 330.

[10] Samuel Sewall, "Diary," Massachusetts Historical Society, *Collections*, fifth series, Vols. V, VI, VII (hereafter Sewall, "Diary," Vols. I, II, III), I, 424.

[11] Sewall, "Diary," III, 233.

[12] Howard, *Matrimonial Institutions*, II, 127; Powell, "Marriage in Early New England", *New England Quarterly*, I, 328; Alice M. Earle, *Customs and Fashions in Old New England*, (New York, 1894), p. 69; see note 50 below.

which required espousals by law was Connecticut. Publication of the banns in that colony consisted of an announcement, eight days in advance, of the intention to enter into a contract of espousals; marriage could not take place until at least another eight days.[13] This requirement did not actually distinguish Connecticut from the rest of New England; for if the other colonies gave no place to the espousal in their law books, it nevertheless formed an accepted part of the business of getting married throughout New England. In Plymouth, Massachusetts, and New Haven, as well as in Connecticut a couple espoused were set apart; they were married as far as other persons were concerned, even though the final ceremony had not taken place. If they could not restrain their sexual impulses, they were forgiven more readily than couples who were not espoused (and the number of cases in which couples confessed to fornication during the period of their espousals suggests that Puritans possessed no more restraint than other human beings).[14] If, after becoming espoused to one person, a man or woman had sexual intercourse with another, the act was considered adultery; and if either party broke the contract without just cause, by refusing to marry the other or by marrying someone else, he might be sued for breach of promise.[15]

In celebrating the wedding after the ceremony the Puritans were no kill-joys. Although they forbade dancing and riotous merry-making on such and all other occasions,[16] they nevertheless considered some sort of feasting to be appropriate. At one espousal Thomas Thatcher defended the proposition that "it is Customary and Commendable to begin with a marriage feast."[17] In accordance with this sentiment, when economy led the General Court of Massachusetts to forbid the sale of cakes and buns in the markets, an

---

[13] *Connecticut Records*, I, 47–48.

[14] See Charles F. Adams, "Some Phases of Sexual Morality and Church Discipline in Colonial New England," Massachusetts Historical Society *Proceedings*, XXVI, 477–516; and Howard, *Matrimonial Institutions*, II, 180–200.

[15] Howard, *Matrimonial Institutions*, II, 180, 200–203.

[16] *Massachusetts Records*, III, 224.

[17] Boston Sermons, Jan. 26, 1674.

exception was made of wedding cakes.[18] From all accounts Puritan weddings were accompanied with plenty of cake, "sackposset," and rum for everyone present.[19]

The final step in marriage was sexual. Unless it were consummated in bodily union, no marriage was complete or valid. If a man proved impotent, his bride was freed from her contract with him. Although New Haven alone made this matter the subject of written law,[20] the Massachusetts records show several cases in which marriages were annulled on account of the husband's impotency.[21] Sexual union constituted the first obligation of married couples to each other, an obligation without the fulfillment of which no persons could be considered married.

The steps leading to marriage reveal something of its duties; the steps that could bring about its dissolution reveal a little more. English law, until 1753, retained the principle of canon law that no marriage can be destroyed. Separations could be obtained for one set of causes and annulments for another, but a separation did not constitute a rupture of the marital bond—neither party could legally remarry—and annulment merely recognized that a particular union had been null and void from the start.[22] In New England, divorce like marriage fell under the jurisdiction of the civil courts and legislatures. Following what they believed to be the laws of God, these courts and legislatures reversed the situation existing in England: they allowed permanent separations under no circumstances, but granted divorce (giving the right to remarry) when either party to a marriage could prove that the other had neglected a fundamental duty. The declaration of some Cambridge ministers reveals what a fundamental duty was:

[18] *Massachusetts Records*, I, 214.

[19] See Alice M. Earle, *Customs and Fashions in Old New England*, p. 73.

[20] *New Haven Records*, p. 586.

[21] George F. Dow, ed., *Records and Files of the Quarterly Courts of Essex County, Massachusetts* 8 vols. (Salem, 1911–21; hereafter *Essex Court Records*), VIII, 356; John Noble et al., eds., *Records of the Court of Assistants of the Colony of the Massachusetts Bay*, 3 vols. (Boston, 1901–28; hereafter *Assistants Records*), III, 67–68.

[22] Howard, *Matrimonial Institutions*, II, 3–117; Powell, *English Domestic Relations 1487–1653*.

QUESTION—In what Cases is a Divorce of the Married justly to be
        Pursued and Obtained?

I. To judge, determine and accomplish a divorce of any married
persons, the civil magistrate is to be addressed or concerned.

II. In case any married persons be found under *natural inca-
pacities,* and *insufficiencies,* which utterly disappoint the confessed
ends of marriage, the marriage is to be declared a nullity.

III. In case any married person be found already bound in a
marriage to another yet living, a divorce is to be granted unto the
aggrieved party.

IV. In case any married person be convicted of such *criminal
uncleanesses* as render them one *flesh* with another obejct than that
unto which their marriage has united them, the injured party may
sue and have their divorce from the offending; which is the plain
sense of the sentence, passed by our Lord, Matth. XIX, 9.

V. In case there be found *incest* in a marriage, a divorce is to
command the separation of the married.

VI. In case, it be found that a person married had, by *fornication*
before marriage, been made *one* with a person related unto the
person with whom they are *now* married, within the degrees made
incestuous by the law of God, it is a just plea for divorce.

VII. In case of a *malicious desertion* by a married person, who
is obliged and invited to return, a divorce may be granted by lawful
authority unto the forsaken. For the word of God is plain, "that a
Christian is not bound in such cases" by the marriage unto one
which has thus wilfully violated the covenant; and tho' our Saviour
forbids "a man's putting away his wife, except it be for fornication,"
yet he forbids not rulers to rescue an innocent person from the
enthralling disadvantages of another that shall sinfully go away.

VIII. As for married persons long absent from each other, and
not heard of by each other, the government may state what *length
of time* in this case, may give such a presumption of *death* in the
person abroad, as may reckon a second marriage free from
scandal.

IX. A divorce being legally pursued and obtained, the innocent
person that is released may proceed unto a "second marriage in the
Lord:" otherwise the state of believers under the New Testament
would in some of these cases be worse than what the God of

heaven directed for his people under the Old.[23]

Though the list makes no distinction between annulment and divorce, obviously several of the causes given were causes for annulment rather than divorce: impotency, near relation to the other party, previous marriage, and previous fornication with a relative of the other party all affected the eligibility of the man or woman to marry; they did not involve neglect to carry out the duties of marriage. When a marriage was dissolved for any of these reasons, it was treated as though it had never existed. For example, when Katherine Ellenwood obtained an annulment because of her husband's impotency, she was given back "her apparel and what estate she brought with her."[24] If she had received a divorce, she would have been entitled to a third of her husband's estate.[25]

The grounds for divorce, as revealed by the statement of the ministers, were adultery, desertion, and absence for a length of time to be determined by the civil government. These were certainly the usual causes for divorce in New England, but in some colonies other neglects of duty could be pleaded in court. Con-

---

[23] Cotton Mather, *Magnalia Christi Americana* (Hartford, 1853), II, 253–254.

[24] *Essex Court Records*, VIII, 356. Another case which illustrated the distinction between annulment and divorce is that of Anna Keayne. Anna married Edward Lane in 1658 and, finding him impotent, sought and obtained an annulment. In 1659 she decided, by what means is not indicated, that Lane was not impotent after all. She and Lane thereupon went to the Governor and asked to be remarried, "but the governor told them that they being separated by the Court it was not for him to Joyne them together; but if they were both sattisfied that the Cause was removed That moved the Court to Declare their Marriage a Nullity . . . That it being Their owne act Their first Marriage was good and the Nullity was voyde." (See E. S. Morgan, "A Boston Heiress and Her Husbands," Colonial Society of Massachusetts *Publications*, XXXIV, 499–513.) This irregular procedure probably could not have been followed if the separation had been a divorce, for the Suffolk County Court made Phillip Wharton and Mary Gridley give bond "to refrain the Company of each other" when they attempted to live together after obtaining a divorce. (Samuel E. Morison and Zechariah Chafee, eds., "Records of the Suffolk County Court, 1671–1680," Colonial Society of Massachusetts *Publications*, XXIX, XXX [hereafter *Suffolk Court Records*], p. 914.)

[25] *Massachusetts Laws of 1648*, p. 17.

necticut allowed divorce for "adultery, fraudulent contract, or willful desertion for three years with totall neglect of duty, or seven years' providentiall absence being not heard of after due enquiry made and certifyed."[26] No cases elucidate the meaning of fraudulent contract; presumably it meant a contract of marriage gained by some kind of fraudulent inducement such as a misrepresentation of financial resources. Total neglect of duty evidently meant failure on the part of the husband to provide economic support for his wife, for three divorces were granted to Connecticut wives for willful desertion and nonsupport by their husbands.[27]

Divorces granted for seven years' providential absence were based on the assumption that anyone absent for seven years could be "counted as legally dead to the other party." The validity of such a divorce would be unimpaired by the subsequent appearance of the absent party who had been supposed dead.[28] Plymouth Colony had no divorce statute, but it granted six divorces in the period during which it existed as a separate colony.[29] Five were for adultery. The sixth was a case of providential absence, in which the court granted the divorce but refused to call it by that name: Mary Atkinson, whose husband had been absent for "the full tearme of seaven yeares and more," was told that "although the Court sees noe cause to graunt a divorce, yett they doe apprehend her to be noe longer bound, but doe leave her to her libertie to marry if shee please."[30] New Haven allowed divorce for adultery and for desertion but made no provision concerning providential absence.[31] Massachusetts passed no divorce laws but granted at least twenty-seven divorces between 1639 and 1692. Of these, thirteen were granted for combined desertion and adultery; for five more no reason was given in the records; the remainder were granted for adultery, cruelty, desertion, long absence, and failure

---

[26] *Connecticut Records*, II, 328.
[27] Ibid., II, 293, 322; III, 23.
[28] Ibid., II, 328.
[29] Howard, *Matrimonial Institutions*, II, 349–351.
[30] *Plymouth Records*, V, 159.
[31] *New Haven Records*, p. 586.

to provide, in such combinations as to make it impossible to tell which was the essential factor.[32] Several petitions deposited in the Massachusetts archives, without indication of whether they were granted or not, requested divorce upon the same grounds.[33]

Court cases involving domestic discord but not divorce give much the same picture of marital duties that the divorce cases do, for the Puritan governments did not always wait for marital troubles to reach the point of divorce without endeavoring to restore harmony and enforce a performance of marital duties. If a husband went off to Barbados or England and never returned, the courts could do nothing about it except to grant a divorce to his wife; but if he refused to live with his wife and remained in New England, he would probably find himself subjected to serious punishment. John Smith of Medfield, for example, who left his wife and went to live with Patience Rawlins, lost ten pounds and gained thirty stripes as a consequence.[34] The same kind of treatment awaited a wife who left home. Mary Drury deserted her husband on the pretence that he was impotent, but she failed to convince the court and had to

---

[32] I have used the convenient list in Howard, *Matrimonial Institutions*, II, 333.

[33] On March 5, 1684/5, for example, Mary Litchfield filed a petition requesting a divorce for her daughter on the ground that the latter's husband had "carried it so wickedly to my Daughter, And so Infidel like, that instead of providing for her tooke from her, her wearing apparrell, And left her almost naked more like an Indian than A Christian swearing most Abominably threatening to split her open, calling my Daughter Mary Dam'd whore, Commanding her to give him his hatt, and several Times beating and abusing her, since which time he hath never come nigh my Daughter nor provided for her, neither for meate, Drinke Cloathing nor Lodging, neither had my Daughter any way to subsist but what she earned for a considerable time by hard working" (from the photostat collection of the Massachusetts Historical Society, March 5, 1684/5). Two weeks later Hannah Eyres petitioned the court for divorce from Benjamin Eyres, whom she had married in England and followed successively to Boston and then to Virginia and finally back to Boston. Each time he had deserted her after a short period and now had fled once more "without the least care to provide for her Notwithstanding what portion he had received with her. . . . And here she is in a farr worse case Than a widdow . . ." (Ibid., March 18, 1684/5).

[34] *Suffolk Court Records*, p. 1158.

pay five pounds.[35] When Ruth Locke left her husband, complaining of ill-treatment, the court admonished them both and ordered her to return.[36] The wife of Phillip Pointing received lighter treatment. When the court thought that she had overstayed her leave in Boston, they simply ordered her "to depart the Towne and goe to Tanton to her husband."[37]

Since marriage was an ordinance of God and its duties commands of God, the Puritan courts enforced these duties not simply at the request of the injured party but on their own paternal initiative. If a man or woman came to Massachusetts and left his mate behind, he would find his stay cut short, unless he had come alone on temporary business or in order to prepare accommodations for his family. Massachusetts laws required that all married persons who had left their consorts in England be shipped back by the next sailing.[38] And the laws were enforced. Persons with wives or husbands in England, as soon as they were discovered, were placed under bond of twenty pounds to return. If they failed to do so, they forfeited the bond but did not gain the right to remain. When Jonathan Atherton forfeited his bond by neglecting several chances to return, the court again ordered "him to return to his wife by the next oppertunity of Shipping under the like penalty."[39] Neither would the court be put off by any improvised excuses. When Paul Hall was "presented for liveing from his wife who is in England, hee appeared in Court and declared that hee was informed that his wife is dead"; but the court "Ordered him to repaire to the Last place of her aboade or bring Certificate that she is dead and pay fees of Court."[40]

The government was not satisfied with mere cohabitation but insisted that it be peaceful. Husbands and wives were forbidden by law to strike each other, and the courts enforced the provision on

[35] Ibid., pp. 837–841.
[36] Ibid., p. 524.
[37] Ibid., p. 121.
[38] *Massachusetts Laws of 1648*, p. 37.
[39] *Suffolk Court Records*, p. 811.
[40] Ibid., p. 23.

numerous occasions.[41] But they did not stop there. Henry Flood was required to give bond for good behavior because he had abused his wife by "ill words calling her whore and cursing of her."[42] The wife of Christopher Collins was presented for railing at her husband and calling him "Gurley gutted divill." Apparently the court agreed with her, for although the fact was proved by two witnesses, she was discharged.[43] On another occasion Jacob Pudeator, who had been fined for striking and kicking his wife, had the sentence moderated when the court was informed that she was a woman "of great provocation."[44]

The duty of a husband to support his wife was also enforced by judicial action. English common law provided that when a woman married, her property passed to her husband and that he must furnish her support. These provisions suited Puritan conceptions, and New England courts enforced them without specific legislative authorization. James Harris was fined ten shillings and required to give bond for good behavior by the Suffolk County Court because of "disorderly carriage in his family neglecting and refuseing to provide for them and for quarrelling with his wife."[45] In the case of William Waters the court gave specific instructions for future behavior:

Upon complaint made to this Court by Elizabeth Waters that her Husband William Waters doth refuse to allow her victuals clothing or fireing necessary for her Support or livelihood and hath acted many unkindnesses and cruelties towards her: The Court having sent for the said William Waters and heard both partys, do Order that the said Waters bee admonish't for his cruelty and unkindness to his wife, and that hee forthwith provide Suitable meate drinke and apparrell for his said wife for future at the Judgement of Mr. Edward Rawson and Mr. Richard Collacot or allow her five Shillings per weeke.[46]

[41] *Massachusetts Laws of 1672*, p. 101; e.g., *Suffolk Court Records*, pp. 88, 114, 116, 330, 867; *Essex Court Records*, V, 221.
[42] *Suffolk Court Records*, p. 410.
[43] *Essex Court Records*, I, 274.
[44] *Ibid.*, V, 377.
[45] *Suffolk Court Records*, p. 307.
[46] *Ibid.*, p. 1063.

In order to prevent adultery, the most grievous cause of divorce, the New England governments did not rely solely upon the dread of capital punishment. To comply with the laws of God, Massachusetts, Connecticut, and New Haven made adultery a capital offense, but they seem to have carried out that punishment only three times. For the most part they sentenced offenders to fines, whippings, brandings, the wearing of a letter "A", and symbolical executions in the form of standing on the gallows with a rope about the neck.[47] Wherever they saw occasion, however, the courts tried to apply the proverbial ounce of prevention rather than wait for the sin to be committed. As early as November 1630 the Court of Assistants prohibited "Mr. Clearke" from "cohabitacion and frequent keepeing company with Mrs. Freeman, under paine of such punishment as the Court shall thinke meete to inflict." Mr. Clark and Mrs. Freeman were both bound "in £XX apeece that Mr. Clearke shall make his personall appearance att the nexte Court to be holden in March nexte, and in the meane tyme to carry himselfe in good behaviour towards all people and espetially towards Mrs. Freeman, concerneing whome there is stronge suspicion of incontinency."[48] Forty-five years later the Suffolk County Court took the same kind of measure to protect the husbands of Dorchester from the temptations offered by the daughter of Robert Spurr. Spurr was presented by the grand jury

for entertaining persons at his house at unseasonable times both by day and night to the griefe of theire wives and Relations &c The Court having heard what was alleaged and testified against him do Sentence him to bee admonish't and to pay Fees of Court and charge him upon his perill not to entertain any married men to keepe company with his daughter especially James Minott and Joseph Belcher.[49]

From such judicial injunctions and legislative enactments as well as from the divorce cases, the fundamental duties of Puritan marriage become apparent: peaceable cohabitation, sexual union and

[47] Howard, *Matrimonial Institutions*, II, 169–174.
[48] *Assistants' Records*, II, 8.
[49] *Suffolk Court Records*, p. 676; see also pp. 442, 443, 1161.

faithfulness, and economic support of the wife by the husband
were essential to the "being" of marriage. But its "well-being," to
use a typical Puritan distinction, required the performance of many
other duties. Fortunately, several persons took the trouble to form-
ulate them in writing, and of course all good Puritans tried to
exemplify them in their daily lives, as their diaries and personal
letters will reveal.

The fullest descriptions of marital ethics were written by Benjamin Wadsworth, Samuel Willard, and John Hull. Hull's contribu-
tion is particularly interesting: it consists of the manuscript notes
which he took of six sermons, five by Thomas Thatcher and one by
John Oxenbridge, all preached at espousal ceremonies and all deal-
ing with the duties of husband and wife.[50] Wadsworth's discussion
of the question is in his *Well Ordered Family* and Willard's in his
exposition of the fifth commandment in *The Compleat Body of
Divinity*. Apart from these specific considerations of the subject
many incidental references to it occur throughout the mass of
doctrinal writing produced in New England in the seventeenth
century. From all these sources, together with diaries and letters, a
more complete picture of Puritan marital ethics emerges.

In seventeenth-century New England no respectable person
questioned that woman's place was in the home. By the laws of
Massachusetts as by those of England a married woman could hold
no property of her own. When she became a wife, she gave up
everything to her husband and devoted herself exclusively to managing his household. Henceforth her duty was to "keep at home,
educating of her children, keeping and improving what is got by
the industry of the man." She was "to see that nothing be *wasted,
or prodigally spent;* that all have what is suitable in due season."[51]
What the husband provided she distributed and transformed to

---

[50] Boston Sermons, Sept. 30, 1672; Aug. 29, 1673; Dec. 30, 1674; Jan. 26,
1674; May 4, 1675; and one undated and labeled "Mr. Thacher at Mr.
wms.' contract." See E. S. Morgan, "Light on the Puritans from John Hull's
Notebooks," *New England Quarterly,* XV (1942), 95–101.

[51] John Cotton, *A Meet Help,* p. 21; Willard, *Compleat Body of Divinity,*
p. 612.

supply the everyday necessities of the family. She turned flour into bread and wool into cloth and stretched the pennies to purchase what she could not make. Sometimes she even took care of the family finances. Samuel Sewall, the famous Puritan diarist, recorded on January 24, 1703/4, that he had turned over the cash account to his wife, relying upon her superior financial judgment:

I paid Capt. Belchar £8–15–0 Took 24s in my pocket, and gave my Wife the rest of my cash £4–3–8, and tell her she shall now keep the Cash; if I want I will borrow of her. She has a better faculty than I at managing Affairs: I will assist her; and will endeavour to live upon my Salary; will see what it will doe. The Lord give his Blessing.[52]

The wife of the Reverend Samuel Whiting showed the same skill as Mrs. Sewall and "by her discretion freed her husband from all *secular avocations*."[53] Similarly when the Reverend Richard Mather's wife died, he thought his affliction "the more grievous, in that she being a Woman of singular Prudence for the Management of Affairs, had taken off from her Husband all Secular Cares, so that he wholly devoted himself to his Study, and to Sacred Imployments."[54]

Whatever financial and managerial ability she might possess, the colonial dame remained subject to her husband's authority. Her place was "to guid the house &c. not guid the Husband."[55] Even in her proper sphere of housewifery she could not rightly have anything "of any great moment disposed of, without his Knowledge and Approbation";[56] in other matters she was expected to depend entirely upon his judgment. Though she clearly possessed the mental powers required for balancing family budgets, she supposedly lacked strength for more serious intellectual exercise. She never attended college, whatever intellectual prowess she might

[52] "Diary," II, 93.

[53] Cotton Mather, *Magnalia Christi Americana* (Hartford, 1853), I, 503.

[54] Increase Mather, *The Life and Death of that Reverend Man of God, Mr. Richard Mather* (Cambridge, 1670), p. 25.

[55] Boston Sermons, Sept. 30, 1672.

[56] Willard, *Compleat Body of Divinity*, p. 612.

display in any secondary school. The accepted estimate of her capacities is revealed in the minister's exhortation to the Puritan husband not only to instruct his wife in religion but "to make it easy to her."[57] She was the weaker vessel in both body and mind, and her husband ought not to expect too much from her. Puritan wives who tried to unsnarl the knotty problems of theology by themselves could take warning from the wife of Governor Hopkins of Connecticut. Mistress Hopkins went insane, and according to Governor Winthrop the reason was that she spent too much time in reading and writing:

Her husband, being very loving and tender of her, was loath to grieve her; but he saw his error, when it was too late. For if she had attended her household affairs, and such things as belong to women, and not gone out of her way and calling to meddle in such things as are proper for men, whose minds are stronger, etc., she had kept her wits, and might have improved them usefully and honorably in the place God had set her.[58]

The fact that she did keep her wits earned no sympathy from the orthodox Puritans for Mrs. Anne Hutchinson. Although she showed considerably more wit than her judges, she was banished from Massachusetts for heresy, and her husband's failure to instruct her properly led Winthrop to call him "a man of a very mild temper and weak parts, and wholly guided by his wife."[59] Another woman who ventured to assert herself by writing a book also fell into heresy and met with rebuke from her brother. Thomas Parker told his sister bluntly, in a public letter: "your printing of a Book, beyond the custom of your Sex, doth rankly smell."[60]

The proper conduct of a wife was submission to her husband's instructions and commands. He was her superior, the head of the

[57] Boston Sermons, Sept. 30, 1672.
[58] John Winthrop, *The History of New England*, James Savage, ed. (Boston, 1853), II, 216.
[59] Ibid., I, 295.
[60] Thomas Parker, *The Coppy of a Letter Written . . . to His Sister* (London, 1650), p. 13.

family, and she owed him an obedience founded on reverence. He
stood before her in the place of God: he exercised the authority of
God over her, and he furnished her with the fruits of the earth that
God had provided. To her and to the rest of the family he was "the
Conduit Pipe of the variety of blessings that God suplyeth them
with."[61] She should therefore look upon him with reverence, a mixture of love and fear, not however "a *slavish Fear*, which is nour-
ished with hatred or aversion; but a *noble* and *generous Fear*,
which proceeds from Love."[62] She was not his slave or his servant.
When Daniel Ela told his wife Elizabeth that "shee was none of his
wife, shee was but his Servantt," neighbors reported the incident to
the authorities, and in spite of the abject Elizabeth's protest "that I
have nothinge Agenst my husband to Charge him with," the Essex
County Court fined him forty shillings.[63]

The Puritan wife of New England occupied a relatively enviable
position by comparison, say, with the wife of early Rome or of the
Middle Ages or even of contemporary England; for her husband's
authority was strictly limited. He could not lawfully strike her, nor
could he command her anything contrary to the laws of God, laws
which were explicitly defined in the civil codes. In one respect she
was almost his equal, for she had "A joint Interest in governing the
rest of their Family." By the logic of relatives she was to children a
parent and to servants a mistress; in relation to them she stood in a
position of authority equal to that of her husband:

If God in his Providence hath bestowed on them Children or
Servants, they have each of them a share in the government of
them; tho' there is an inequality in the degree of this Authority,
and the Husband is to be acknowledged to hold a *Superiority*,
which the Wife is practically to allow; yet in respect of all others in
the Oeconomical Society, she is invested with an Authority over
them by God; and her Husband is to allow it to her, and the others
are to carry it to her as such: Touching *Children*, the *letter* of the

[61] *Boston Sermons*, Sept. 30, 1672.
[62] Willard, *Compleat Body of Divinity*, p. 612.
[63] *Essex Court Records*, VIII, 272, 273 (March 1682).

Command expresseth it; and it is urged elsewhere with *Emphasis,* as we formerly observed: And as to *Servants,* the Metaphorical and Synecdochical usage of the words *Father* and *Mother,* heretofore observed, implys it; for tho' the Husband be the Head of the Wife, yet she is an Head of the Family.[64]

In accordance with this conception, Samuel Sewall advised his son's servant Tom that "he could not obey his Master without obedience to his Mistress; and *vice versa,*"[65] a piece of advice that Tom may have found perplexing, for a dispute was in progress between the younger Sewall and his wife. In the course of it, the elder Sewall made the following laconic note in his diary:

Oct. 30, [1713] Sam. and his Wife dine here, go home together in the Calash. William Ilsly rode and pass'd by them. My son warn'd him not to lodge at his house; Daughter said she had as much to doe with the house as he. Ilsly lodged there.[66]

It was wrong for Sam's wife thus to flaunt him, but her assertion of her rights was not without foundation.

When married life was properly ordered, however, the wife could have no just occasion to complain, for a good husband would "make his government of her, as easie and gentle as possible; and strive more to be lov'd than fear'd; though neither is to be excluded."[67] Such ideal government on the part of the husband was supposed to produce a joyful submission in the wife. Samuel Willard says that a husband should so rule "as that his Wife may take delight in it, and not account it a Slavery, but a Liberty and Priviledge; and the Wife ought to carry it so to her Husband, as he may take Content in her: And whatsoever is contrary to this, and is rendred grievous to either Party, deriveth not from the Precept, but from the Corruption there is in the Hearts of Men."[68] The reverent submission which Willard was trying to describe here can best be illustrated by

[64] Willard, *Compleat Body of Divinity,* p. 610.
[65] "Diary," II, 370–371.
[66] "Diary," II, 405–406.
[67] Benjamin Wadsworth, *The Well-Ordered Family,* p. 36.
[68] Willard, *Compleat Body of Divinity,* p. 612.

a passage from a letter of gentle Margaret Winthrop to her husband, written when he was absent in London. She tells him of a brief journey she is planning to make to visit some relatives while he is gone, and then adds: "Thou seast how bold I am to take leave to goe abrode in thy abcence, but I presume upon thy love and concent, or elce I wolde not doe it. I hope I shall take order that all thinges shalbe wel looked to for the time I stay." She goes on to send him her "best love and all due respect . . . which my pen can not exprese or my tongue utter, but I will endevor to shew it as well as I can to thee, and to all that love thee." She signs the letter as usual, "your faythful and obedient wife Margaret Winthrope."[69]

In describing the husband's authority and the wife's submission it has been necessary again and again to use the word "love." Love was indeed, as one minister put it, "the Sugar to sweeten every addition to married life but not an essential part of it. Love was Condition in the married Relation,"[70] but it was more than sugar. The minister did not mean to imply that love was a luxury, a happy more than a fortunate accident to the Puritans. It was a duty imposed by God on all married couples. It was a solemn obligation that resulted directly from the marriage contract. If husband and wife failed to love each other above all the world, they not only wronged each other, they disobeyed God. *The Great God commands thee to love her,"* exclaimed Wadsworth. "How vile then are those who don't love their Wives." Wadsworth further explained:

This duty of love is mutual, it should be performed by each, to each of them. They should endeavour to have their affections really, cordially and closely knit, to each other. If therefore the *Husband* is bitter against his wife, beating or striking of her (as some vile wretches do) or in any unkind carriage, ill language, hard words, morose, peevish, surly behaviour; nay if he is not kind, loving, tender in his words and carriage to her; he then shames his profession of Christianity, he breaks the Divine Law, he dishonours God

---

[69] Robert C. Winthrop, *The Life and Letters of John Winthrop* (Boston, 1869), I, 299.

[70] Sewall, "Diary," II, 403.

and himself too, by this ill behaviour. The same is true of the *Wife* too. If she strikes her Husband (as some shameless, impudent wretches will) if she's unkind in her carriage, give ill language, is sullen, pouty, so cross that she'l scarce eat or speak sometimes; nay if she neglects to manifest real love and kindness, in her words or carriage either; she's then a shame to her profession of Christianity, she dishonours and provokes the glorious God, tramples his Authority under her feet; she not only affronts her Husband, but also God her Maker, Lawgiver and Judge, by this her wicked behaviour. The indisputable Authority, the plain Command of the Great God, required Husbands and Wives, to have and manifest very great affection, love and kindness to one another. They should (out of Conscience to God) study and strive to render each others life, easy, quiet and comfortable; to please, gratifie and oblige one another, as far as lawfully they can.[71]

In spite of these views the ministers hastened to warn husbands and wives that their love for each other required moderation. The highest love of all Christians was reserved for God himself; and since human beings, husbands and wives, were only the creatures of God, they could not take his place. Every benefit and comfort obtained from them came ultimately from him. To prize them too highly was to upset the order of creation and descend to idolatry. When we take too much pleasure in any creature, "when we exceedingly delight our selves in Husbands, or Wives, or Children," it "much benumbs and dims the light of the Spirit." Man and wife forgot their maker when they were "so transported with affection," that they aimed "at no higher end than marriage it self." True conjugal affection demanded that "such as have wives look at them not for their own ends, but to bee better fitted for Gods service, and bring them nearer to God."[72]

Human mortality gave grim warning to every Puritan couple that God had placed a limit on their love, for marriage ended at the grave. There would be "no marrying in Heaven,"[73] only the blessed

---

[71] *Well-Ordered Family*, pp. 25, 36.

[72] John Cotton, *Practical Commentary upon John*, pp. 126, 200.

[73] Thomas Hooker, *A Comment upon Christ's Last Prayer*, p. 193.

communion of saints, each of whom would be "as dear to another, as if all relations of husbands, and wives, of parents, and children, and friends, were in every one of them."[74] When a widow or widower showed immoderate grief, he showed that he had not kept his love within bounds. He showed that he had valued a creature too highly. Therefore, although the minister urged married couples to love each other above everything and everybody else in the world, he always warned them to "let this caution be minded, that they dont love inordinately, because death will soon part them."[75] Whenever death did part or threaten to part a Puritan couple, the survivor could seldom refrain from meditating upon whether he had maintained the proper moderation in his affections. After Thomas Shepard's wife had almost died in childbirth, he reflected that "as the affliction was very bitter so the Lord did teach me much by it, and I had need of it for I began to grow secretly proud and full of sensuality delighting my soule in my deare wife more then in my god whom I had promised better unto." When Shepard's wife did die several years later, he observed that "this made me resolve to delight no more in creatures but in the Lord."[76] The wife of Reverend Jonathan Burr found it difficult to maintain so philosophical an attitude at her husband's deathbed, but he rebuked her sternly: "Don't spend so much time with me, but go thy way and spend some time in prayer: thou knowest not what thou mayst obtain from God; I fear lest thou look too much upon this affliction."[77] If a widow or widower failed to make the proper reflection himself, someone else would make it in a letter of condolence. Thus when the Lady Mary Vere lost her husband, John Davenport wrote: "The relation which once you had to this earthly husband is ended, and ceaseth in his death, but the relation you have to our heavenly husband remayneth inviolable. . . . So that it

[74] John Davenport, *The Saints Anchor-Hold in all Storms and Tempests* (London, 1682), p. 28.

[75] Wadsworth, *Well-Ordered Family*, p. 26.

[76] "Autobiography," in Colonial Society of Massachusetts *Publications*, XXVII, 374, 395.

[77] Cotton Mather, *Magnalia*, I, 374.

is but a conduit pipe that is broken; the fountaine being still open to you." When Lady Vere's daughter also became a widow, Davenport in the same vein expressed his hopes to her "that the mortality of earthly comforts, and the dissoublenes of the marriage bond with the creature may quicken us to secure our interest in the everliving God, and our marriage with the Lord J. C. by an everlasting convenant of his free grace, which nothing can dissolve."[78]

Good Puritans controlled their affections even in love letters. Edward Taylor, the minister of Westfield, Conn., began an ardent message to his sweetheart with these words: "My Dove, I send you not my heart, for that I trust is sent to Heaven long since, and unless it hath wofully deceived me, it hath not taken up its lodgings in any one's bosom on this side of the Royal City of the Great King, but yet most of it that is allowed to be layed out upon any creature doth safely and singly fall to your share." After this caution he went on to describe his passion for her as "a golden ball of pure fire" and to explain "that Conjugall love ought to exceed all other," yet he could not refrain from adding that "it must be kept within bounds too. For it must be subordinate to Gods Glory."[79] The letters of John and Margaret Winthrop also illustrate the orthodox conception of conjugal love.[80] When the couple had been espoused, John addressed his bride-to-be as "the happye and hopeful supplie (next Christ Jesus) of my greatest losses." In the first letter that is preserved after the time of their marriage, he saluted her as "the chiefest of all comforts under the hope of Salvation, which hope cannot be valued," and he prayed "that these earthly blessings of mariage, healthe, friendship, etc, may increase our estimation of our better and onely ever duringe happinesse in heaven." In the next letter he wrote, "My sweet spouse, let us delight in the love of eache other as the chiefe of all earthly comforts." This was the

---

[78] Isabel MacB. Calder, ed., *Letters of John Davenport* (New Haven, 1937), pp. 58, 77.

[79] Frances M. Caulkins, *History of Norwich, Connecticut* (Hartford, 1866), p. 154.

[80] The quotations which follow are taken from Winthrop, *Life and Letters of John Winthrop*, I, 135, 159, 161, 261, 290; II, 179.

leitmotif of all the letters that followed. John and Margaret delighted in each other as long as life kept them together, but they never valued their love as more than an "earthly" comfort. In May 1628, when John had been absent for an especially long period in London and had undergone sickness there, Margaret wrote him resignedly: "Thus it pleaseth the Lord to exercise us with one affliction after another in love; lest we should forget our selves and love this world too much, and not set our affections on heaven wheare all true happyness is for ever." A year later her husband philosophized in another absence: "We see how frail and vain all earthly good things are. There is no means to avoid the loss of them in death, nor the bitterness which accompanyeth them in the cares and troubles of this life. Only the fruition of Jesus Christ and the hope of heaven can give us true comfort and rest." On the occasion of the Antinomian controversy in Boston, John was forced to part from his wife again for a brief time and took the opportunity to send her the last letter of any length that has been preserved from their correspondence. It is written in the same key as all that preceded: "Deare [torn], I am still detayned from thee, but it is by the Lord, who hath a greater interest in me than thy selfe, when his worke is donne he will restore me to thee againe to our mutuall comfort: Amen."

Not all Puritan couples had to worry about limiting their affection. Many found it more difficult to love each other enough than to keep their love within bounds. Love could be a difficult business, demanding all the attention and care a man could give it; for human depravity, according to the Puritans, had so deprived man of control over his affections that it was not easy for him to direct his love to the proper objects in the proper proportions. Human corruption sowed many seeds of irritation, seeds which would grow and split every bond of love if they were not rooted out with the greatest patience. The Puritan's consciousness of these dangers helped him to avoid them. By recognizing that conjugal love was "very difficult because of your many infirmities," it became easier to exercise "Patience and meekness forbearing forgiving and forgeting Provocations." "If offences be," said Thomas Thatcher, "you must not dwell upon them nor repeate them but Cross scores every night under pain of giving place to the divell, to remember Past offences will separate dearest freinds it is enough to bear our owne burthens of the day in the day, god forgives us dayly so must wee."[81]

Some of the advice offered to these reluctant lovers was not far different from that given to the more ardent kind, the kind who found difficulty in restraining their love within proper bounds. "Look not for Perfection in your relation," Thatcher advised one couple. "God reserves that for another state where marriage is not needed." Thatcher could easily have proceeded from such a premise to a warning against making human love an end in itself, against exalting the creature above God. Instead he launched into an exhortation to the couple before him to "exercise Patience and meekness in all losses and crosses in this life."[82] The very limitation of marital love assisted frail human beings to attain it. Conjugal happiness, John Oxenbridge explained, was furthered "by limitting the expectation," by remembering that "you mary a child of Adam,"[83] in other words by not expecting to obtain from the creature the bliss which God alone could give. Thus the proper ordering of conjugal love, in accordance with the order of creation, provided the remedy for excess and defect alike.

Puritan love, then, was no romantic passion but a rational love, in which the affections were commanded by the will under the guidance of the reason. To be sure, human depravity violated the order of creation: frequently the affections took the bit in their teeth and rebelled and could hardly be brought under control by the will. But in their proper place the affections were only "under servants to the Soul."[84] When Benjamin Thompson wished to praise the Reverend Samuel Whiting, he wrote:

[81] Boston Sermons, Sept. 30, 1672, and May 4, 1675.
[82] Boston Sermons, Sept. 30, 1672.
[83] Boston Sermons, August 24, 1673.
[84] John Eliot, *The Harmony of the Gospels* (Boston, 1678), p. 70. Cf. Perry Miller, *The New England Mind: The Seventeenth Century*, ch. ix.

> Church doctors are my witnesses, that here
> Affections always kept their proper sphere,
> Without those wilder eccentricities,
> Which spot the fairest fields of men most wise.[85]

When affections kept their proper sphere, a lover did not display that divine—or to the Puritans diabolical—madness admired in the cult of romantic love; instead he allowed his reason to choose the object of his love and then commanded his affections to act accordingly. Thus when Michael Wigglesworth wished to persuade the pious Mrs. Avery to marry him, he did not lay claim to any violent passion for her. He wrote her a letter carefully listing ten reasons why she should marry him and answering two objections which she had raised to the match. His first reason was that after a short meeting with her "my thoughts and heart have been toward you ever since." But the rest of the reasons make it clear that he did not mean to suggest in this first one that his was a case of love at first sight, according to the pattern familiar to us:

2ly. That upon serious, earnest and frequent seeking of God for guidance and Direction in so weighty a matter, my thoughts have still been determined unto and fixed upon yourself as the most suitable Person for me.

3ly. In that I have not been led hereunto by fancy (as too many are in like cases) but by sound Reason and judgment, Principally Loving and desiring you for those gifts and graces God hath bestowed upon you, and Propounding the Glory of God, the adorning and furtherance of the Gospel. The spiritual as wel as outward good of myself and family, together with the good of yourself and children, as my Ends inducing me hereunto.

The remainder of the reasons were all directed to proving that it would be convenient and comfortable for her to marry him, which she did.[86]

A similar attitude is revealed, though in the more stilted lan-

---

[85] Cotton Mather, *Magnalia*, I, 510.
[86] *New England Historical and Genealogical Register*, XVII, 140–142.

guage of the eighteenth century, by the diary of the Reverend
Samuel Dexter:

> Nov. 22, 1723. I Communicated something of my mind to the
> young Lady, which I hope (and I think I have reason to hope) may
> thro' the smiles of Indulgent Providence be the Person in whom I
> may find that good thing and obtain favour of the Lord. I think
> I have not been rash in my proceedings—she is as far as I Can find
> a Woman of Merit—a woman of good Temper and of prudent Con-
> duct and Conversation.[87]

Puritan love as revealed in the preceding passages was not so
much the cause as it was the product of marriage. It was the chief
duty of husband and wife toward each other, but it did not necessarily form a sufficient reason for marriage. Wadsworth advised no
one to marry any person for any reason *"unless they can have a
real cordial love to them;* for God strictly commands *mutual love* in
this Relation."[88] The advice was not that couples should not marry
unless they *love* each other but that they should not marry unless
they *can* love each other. Corrupt human nature sometimes prevented a couple from ever attaining affection for each other; therefore care should be taken to match with someone whom you would
find it possible to love. But that you should love in advance was by
no means essential.

As a matter of fact, Puritan diaries and letters suggest that the
decision to marry was usually made by a man or woman without
reference to any particular match. Thomas Shepard, for example,
made up his mind to get married before he had a prospect in sight,
for he wrote in his autobiography: ". . . now, about this time I had
a great desire to change my estate by marriage; and I had bin pray-
ing 3 yeare before that the Lord would carry me to such a place
where I might have a meet yoke fellow. . . .[89] Thomas Walley
showed less concern than Shepard about finding a suitable mate.
Once he had decided to get married, finding a wife was simply a

---

[87] *New England Historical and Genealogical Register*, XIV, 40.
[88] *Well-Ordered Family*, p. 42.
[89] Colonial Society of Massachusetts *Publications*, XXVII, 370.

matter of going to Boston, and even that inconvenience was spared him by a lucky chance. He wrote to his friend John Cotton, telling him of his good fortune; the letter is dated Sept. 20, 1675:

As for my Journey to Boston it is spoiled. god hath sent me a wife home to me and saved m[e] the labor of a tediouse Journey. the last day of the last week I came to a resolve to stay at home and not to look after a wife till the spring. the next morning I heard Mrs. Clark of the Iland was come to our Towne who had bin mentioned by some of my friends. the providence of God hath soe ordered it that we are agreed to become one.[90]

After a man had decided to enter the married estate, he had to face the problem of choosing a mate. Love, as already noted, had little to do with the matter. The most important factor affecting the choice was the social rank of the persons involved. The ministers warned that "the happiness of marige life consists much in that Persons being equally yoaked draw together in a holy yoak . . . there must be sutable fittness for this Condition equality in birth, education and religion,"[91] to which might have been added equality in wealth. The affections should not be allowed to attach themselves to anyone of a different social status, and if one were a church member, he should not allow his eyes to roam outside the church. After Wigglesworth's first wife died, he lost control of himself and married his serving maid. Before the event took place, the rumor of it brought prompt rebuke from his former pupil, Increase Mather: "The Report is, that you are designing to marry with your servant mayd, and that she is one of obscure parentage, and not over 20 years old, and of no Church, nor so much as Baptised. If it be as is related, I would humbly entreat you (before it be too late) to consider of these arguments in opposition." The arguments were: (1) that it would be a great grief to his relations, (2) that it would shorten his life, (3) that it would injure his reputation, (4) that it

[90] Curwin Papers (manuscripts in the library of the American Antiquarian Society at Worcester, Massachusetts), III, 46.

[91] Boston Sermons, no date given, probably 1673 or 1674. The sermon is headed "Mr. Thacher at Mr. wms' Contract."

would injure the reputation of the whole ministry, and (5) that it would break the rule of marrying equals. "The like never was in N. E.," said Mather, "Nay, I question whether the like hath bin known in the christian world." And he added a bit of practical advice: "Though your affections should be too far gone in this matter, I doubt not but if you put the object out of your sight, and looke up to the Lord Jesus for supplies of grace, you will be enabled to overcome these Temptacions."[92]

The problem of matching with an equal became a difficult one for Hugh Hall, whose father had moved from New England to Barbados but sent his son back to Harvard for education. When Hugh had completed his education, he returned to Barbados and, entering his father's business, became increasingly prosperous. During a return visit to Boston in 1718, he wrote back to his father that "it will be high time for me upon my Return to You, to think of the Conjugal State; and I Presume it may not be Amiss to get a Private Information of the Quantum of Mrs. P . . . . y (if Mr. H—n dont Address her) and how the Pulse of the Family would beat at my Application." Apparently the quantum was not sufficient or else the pulse of the family did not beat favorably, or perhaps Mr. H—n got there first. At any rate a year later Hugh wrote from Barbados back to Benjamin Emmons in Boston that

from the Satisfaction I take in a Batcheldors Life am very maturely Deliberating whether I had best Commence the Matrimonial State or no, which if it should happen in the Affirmative, I Conjecture I shall be as much Plunged where to make my Application; for I shall be pretty Difficult under my present Circumstances, and much more if I Arrive to be a Ten Thousand pound Man, which I doubt not a few Years will Effect (GOD Sparing my Life). . . .[93]

There is no evidence as to how Hugh solved his problems, but the records which survive of the negotiations preceding other matches show that in many cases the wooing of a lady consisted largely in financial bargaining. In the case of widows and widowers the hag-

[92] Massachusetts Historical Society *Collections*, fourth series, VIII, 94–95.
[93] Manuscript Letterbook in the Harvard College Library, pp. 92, 176.

gling took place directly between the parties concerned, but in most first marriages the parents fought out the sordid pecuniary details while the children were left to the business of knitting their affections to each other. The latter process, however, was usually supposed to follow rather than precede the financial agreement. Parental consent was legally required for a first marriage, and parental consent usually depended upon the attainment of a satisfactory bargain with the parents of the other party, each side endeavoring to persuade the other to give a larger portion to the young couple. A letter of Fitz-John Winthrop to his brother shows how economic considerations might affect the choice of a mate. "I think," said Fitz-John, who had been consulted about a bride for his nephew,

there is little to be thought about it except in one extreeme:—as if a man should be [so] unhapy [as] to dote upon a poore wench (tho' otherwise well enough) that would reduce him to necessety and visibly ruine his common comforts and reputation, and at the same time there should be recommended to him a goodly lass with aboundation of mony which would carry all before it, give him comfort, and inlarge his reputation and intrest. I would certainly, out of my sense of such advantage to my freind, advise him to leave the maid with a short hempen shirt, and take hold of that made of good bag holland.[94]

Such a statement may be thought to reflect a mercenary spirit which had crept into Puritanism by the end of the century, but a letter of Emmanuel Downing to the first John Winthrop in 1643 displays a similar attitude:

For my Cosen Deane's busines, I see no lett nor hindrance but yt may proceede with as much expedition as you please, without any further delay then modesty requireth in such occasions. the portion, as I understand, is about £200. If you be content therewith, I suppose the quality and person of the mayde will not give cause of dislike.[95]

[94] Massachusetts Historical Society *Collections*, sixth series, III, 396. The letter is dated Aug. 28, 1707.
[95] *Winthrop Papers*, IV, 439.

Another letter, from Lucy Downing to John Winthrop in 1641 concerned an attempt to match her son James with Rebecca Cooper, a ward of Governor Endicott's. After asking Winthrop's assistance in persuading Endicott to the match, she wrote:

The disposition of the mayde and her education with Mrs. Endicot are hopefull, her person tollerable and the estate very convenient, and that is the state of the business. allso James is incouraged by the mayds frinds to prosecute the sute, but I think he hath not yet spoken to the mayd as I hear.[96]

Obtaining Rebecca's consent was obviously a minor matter as compared with the acquisition of her estate, for her person was only "tollerable," while her estate was "very convenient."

In the case of second marriages the bargaining over estates played a more direct part in the procedure of courtship. It has often been observed that widows were popular in colonial New England. The reason was that a widow in New England, as in England, inherited a life estate in at least a third of all the land which her husband had possessed at any time during their marriage,[97] a larger proportion than he could usually afford to give a single child as a marriage portion either during his life or after his death. Since the husband obtained the usufruct of his wife's property, every man aspired to get as much property with his wife as possible, and widows usually had the most to offer. Sewall was aiming high when he sought the hand of Wait Winthrop's widow, but she proved a better bargainer than he. She demanded that he keep a coach if she should agree to marry him. Sewall felt that he could not afford to keep a coach, that the estate which he would gain by her would not make it worthwhile, and so he broke off negotiations. When such negotiations were successful, a widow usually stipulated in a prenuptial contract that she should retain the title to any part of her former husband's estate that descended to her by will, with the right to dispose of it by a last will and testament of her own.

---

[96] *Winthrop Papers*, IV, 303.

[97] George L. Haskins, *Law and Authority in Early Massachusetts* (New York, 1960), pp. 180–182.

(Her widow's third reverted to her former husband's heirs at her death.)[98] The new husband thus acquired only the yearly income of her property, but even that sufficed to give a widow the choice of several suitors.

Marriage then, or at least proper marriage, resulted not from falling in love, but from a decision to enter a married state, followed by the choice of a suitable person. But since love formed the chief duty of marriage and since the unruly affections of fallen man might sometimes fail at once to knit themselves to the chosen object, a period of trial was necessary in which to bring the affections into the proper direction. That period was furnished by the custom of espousals. "By this meanes," said William Ames, "the minds of the betroathed, are prepared and disposed to those affections, which in matrimony are requisite";[99] and Thomas Welde wrote in his commonplace book that "Everie Marriage before it be knit, should be contracted. as is shewed. Exod. 22. 16 and Deut. 22. 28. which stay between the contract and the marriage, was the time of longing, for the affections to settle in. . . ."[100] When John Winthrop had been contracted to Margaret Tyndal, he wrote her tender letters expressing his longing for her and his earnest endeavor to rest his affections wholly upon her. Bold man that he was, he suggested that she help him by refraining from the extravagant fashions and ornamentations of the period and explained that "the great and sincere desire which I have that there might be no discouragement to daunt the edge of my affections, whyle they are truly labouring to settle and repose themselves in thee, makes me thus watchfull and jealous of the least occasion that Sathan might stirr up to our discomfort."[101]

It might be supposed that these self-conscious efforts would turn

---

[98]. For two such agreements see the *New England Historical and Genealogical Register*, XII, 353, and Massachusetts Historical Society, *Collections*, sixth series, V, 154–160.

[99] *Conscience, with the Power and Cases Thereof* (London, 1643), Book V, p. 204.

[100] Manuscript in the library of the Massachusetts Historical Society, p. 87.

[101] Winthrop, *Life and Letters of John Winthrop*, I, 137.

out a dry form of love indeed, but the facts belie the supposition. The love which proceeded from Christian charity, conceived in reason and conscious of God's sacred order, was warm and tender and gracious. The letters of John and Margaret Winthrop display an emotion which is all the more convincing because of its sincere restraint and lack of hyperbole. No one could call the love dry or ascetic which produced the following lines from Margaret when her husband was attending court in London: "I will not looke for any longe letters this terme because I pitty your poore hande; if I had it heere I would make more of it than ever I did, and bynde it up very softly for fear of hurting it." John usually closed his letters with phrases such as these: "I kiss and love thee with the kindest affection, and rest Thy faithful husband"; "so I kisse thee and wish thee Farewell"; "I kisse my sweet wife and remaine allwayes thy faithfull husband"; "many kisses of Love I sende thee: farewell"; "so with the sweetest kisses, and pure imbracinges of my kindest affection I rest Thine." The possibility of achieving truly lovely feelings towards another person by force of will is demonstrated in a letter which John's father wrote to Margaret at the time of her espousal and before he (the father) had ever met her. Though it is not of course an example of conjugal love, it helps to throw light upon the manner in which a true Christian might direct his affections toward one with whom he had entered into close relation. I quote only the opening sentence, but the whole letter possesses the same quality:

I am, I assure you, (Gentle Mistress Margaret) alredy inflamed with a fatherly Love and affection towardes you: the which at the first, the only report of your modest behaviour, and mielde nature, did breede in my heart; but nowe throughe the manifest tokens of your true love, and constant minde, which I perceyve to be setteled in you towardes my soonne, the same is exceedingly increased in mee.[102]

Other Puritan writings demonstrate that the Winthrops were not

[102] The quotations in this paragraph are all from Winthrop, *Life and Letters of John Winthrop*, I, 261, 291, 292, 197, 161, 163, 127.

an exceptional case. Ann Bradstreet's poems have the same depth and sincerity of affection as the Winthrop letters. The titles alone indicate the kind of feeling that produced them: "To my Dear and loving Husband," "For the restoration of my dear Husband from a burning Ague," "Upon my dear and loving Husband his goeing into England," "In my Solitary houres in my dear husband his Absence," "In thankfull acknowledgment for the letters I received from my husband out of England," "In thankfull Remembrance for my dear husbands safe Arrival."[103]

The metaphorical imagery of Puritan theological works, especially those of Thomas Hooker, displays a singular sensitivity to the warmth of conjugal love. The relation of husband and wife furnished the usual metaphor by which the relation of Christ and the believer was designated.[104] In elaborating that metaphor Hooker showed that Puritan love, despite its restraint and care for the order of God, could delight the lovers as much as any love. The proper accompaniment to the Winthrop letters is Hooker's delineation of the ordinances of the church as Christ's love-letters:

As a wife deales with the letters of her husband that is in a farre Country; she finds many sweet inklings of his love, and shee will read these letters often, and daily: she would talke with her husband a farre off, and see him in the letters, Oh (saith she) thus and thus hee thought when he writ these lines, and then she thinkes he speaks to her againe; she reads these letters only, because she would be with her husband a little, and have a little parley with him in his pen, though not in his presence: so these ordinances are but the Lords love-letters. . . .

Hooker's picture of a husband is equally charming:

The man whose heart is endeared to the woman he loves, he dreams of her in the night, hath her in his eye and apprehension when he awakes, museth on her as he sits at table, walks with her

---

[103] John H. Ellis, ed., *Works of Anne Bradstreet* (Charlestown, Mass., 1867; New York, 1932), passim.
[104] See ch. VII below.

when he travels and parlies with her in each place where he comes. . . .

That the Husband tenders his Spouse with an indeared affection above al mortal creatures: This appeares by the expressions of his respect, that all he hath, is at her command, al he can do, is wholly improved for her content and comfort, she lies in his Bosom, and his heart trusts in her, which forceth al to confess, that the stream of his affection, like a mighty current, runs with ful Tide and strength. . . .

The fact that these passages appear in a metaphorical description of the relation between man and God does not weaken the obvious authenticity of their language. Hooker was describing feelings that really existed, and in another passage he showed that he thought that these feelings arose in the orthodox manner: "If a woman," he wrote, "have with a conjugall affection taken a man to be her husband, that same taking of him to be her husband, makes her love him. . . ."[105]

The Puritans have gained from their modern descendants a reputation for asceticism that is not easily dispelled. Yet if we are to believe their own statements, they never thought of marriage as a purely spiritual partnership. When John Cotton had joined a couple in matrimony in 1694, he preached a sermon to them in which he recalled the case of

one who immediately upon Marriage, without ever approaching the *Nuptial Bed,* indented with the *Bride,* that by mutual consent they might both live such a life, and according did sequestring themselves according to the custom of those times, from the rest of mankind, and afterwards from one another too, in their retired Cells, giving themselves up to a Contemplative life; and this is recorded as an Instance of no little or ordinary Vertue; but I must be pardoned in it, if I can account it no other than an effort of blind zeal, for they are the dictates of a blind mind they follow therein,

[105] The quotations from Hooker are taken from *The Soules Humiliation* (London, 1638), pp. 73–74; *The Application of Redemption* (London, 1659), p. 137; *A Comment upon Christ's Last Prayer* (London, 1656), p. 187; and *The Saints Dignitie and Dutie* (London, 1651), p. 5.

and not of that Holy Spirit, which saith *It is not good that man should be alone.*[106]

Benjamin Wadsworth showed the same attitude: he advised married couples not to let quarrels "make you live separately, nor lodge separately neither: for if it once comes to this, Satan has got a great advantage against you, and tis to be fear'd he'l get a greater."[107] So thoroughly had these ideas permeated Puritan society that Edmund Pinson complained to the Middlesex County Court because Richard Dexter had slandered him by saying "that he Brock his deceased wife's hart with Greife, that he wold be absent from her 3 weeks together when he was at home, and wold never come nere her, and such Like."[108]

As a matter of fact the Puritans were a much earthier lot than their modern critics have imagined. It is well to remember that they belonged to the age in which they lived and not to the more squeamish decades of the nineteenth or twentieth centuries (the only edition of John Winthrop's *Journal* printed in the twentieth century is expurgated). Seaborn Cotton, son of New England's leading divine, while a student at Harvard College started a notebook in which he copied some of the more explicit passages from Elizabethan and Cavalier love poems. When he later became minister of the church at Hampton, New Hampshire, he saw no incongruity in using the same copybook to take notes of church meetings. The record of one meeting in 1663 follows a receipt "For to make a handsom woman."[109] A similar disregard for the proprieties so dear to another century characterized a letter sent by John Haynes to Fitz-John Winthrop in 1660. Both men belonged to orthodox and honored New England families, and the writer had graduated from Harvard College four years before. The letter indicates that Haynes had been commissioned to buy a pair of garters for Winthrop to

---

[106] *A Meet Help*, p. 16.
[107] *Well-Ordered Family*, p. 33.
[108] Middlesex Files, folder 42, group 3 (October 1666).
[109] Samuel E. Morison, *Harvard College in the Seventeenth Century* (Cambridge, 1937), pp. 126–132.

present to his fiancée. This in itself would have shocked a generation instructed in the notion that ladies have no legs, but Haynes was not embarrassed. In sending his compliments to the lady, he wrote: "I do not say I am fond of the happynes to kiss her hands, but her feet, having interest in her legs till my Garters be payd, which I adjure you to be carefull of as you would be glad to have a Lady leggs and all."[110]

In short, the Puritans were neither prudes nor ascetics. They knew how to laugh, and they knew how to love. But it is equally clear that they did not spend their best hours in either love or laughter. They had fixed their eyes on a heavenly goal, which directed and informed their lives. When earthly delights dimmed their vision, it was time to break off. Yet even this side of the goal there was room for joy.

[110] Massachusetts Historical Society *Proceedings*, XXI, 123. See also E. S. Morgan, "The Puritans and Sex," *New England Quarterly*, XV (1942), 591–607.

III

Parents
and Children

*T*HE first duty of a Puritan parent was the duty of any parent: to give food, shelter, and protection to his children. The Puritans read this lesson in the book of nature. "Even the bruit Creatures, and those that are most Savage," Joseph Belcher pointed out, "are carried by a natural instinct towards those that issue and proceed from them. They Feed and Nourish, and take care of, and protect their young Ones."[1] The laws obliged all parents to perform this duty: no New England father could loaf away his time while the cupboard was bare. When a complaint was made in Watertown against Hugh Parsons, "he was Sent For, and advised to imploy his time to the better providing For his Family, and for his incouragment" he was supplied "with some present Corne."[2] Other offenders received shorter shrift. Samuel Mattock, indicted by the grand jury of Suffolk "for Idleness and neglecting his Family," was sentenced "to bee sent to the house of correction for an idle person and to pay Fees of Court."[3] Moreover, the courts demanded that children be given more care than the mere provision of food and shelter. The Essex County Court in September 1660 admonished Francis Urselton and his wife "for leaving their children alone in the night in a lonely house, far from neighbors, after having been warned of

---

[1] Joseph Belcher, *Two Sermons Preached in Dedham* (Boston, 1710), p. 2.
[2] *Watertown Records* (Watertown, 1894), I, 64.
[3] *Suffolk Court Records*, p. 231. See also pp. 89, 259, 306, 721, 753, 835, 844, 846, 870, 957.

it," and fourteen years later did the same to John Downing's wife, who was "Presented for neglecting their children, some days and nights, often leaving them alone."[4]

A parent had to provide for his children, because they were unable to provide for themselves. If he was ever to free himself of the obligation, he must see to it that they knew how to earn a living. "If you're careful to bring them up diligently in proper business," Benjamin Wadsworth advised parents, "you take a good method for their comfortable subsistence in this World (and for their being serviceable in their Generation) you do better for them, then if you should bring them up idly, and yet leave them great Estates."[5] According to law every father had to see that his children were instructed "in some honest lawful calling, labour or imployment, either in husbandry, or some other trade profitable for themselves, and the Common-wealth if they will not or cannot train them up in learning to fit them for higher imployments."[6]

For the first few years of a child's life he was not seriously disturbed by the process of learning a calling. John Cotton did not consider it idleness for young children to "spend much time in pastime and play, for their bodyes are too weak to labour, and their minds to study are too shallow . . . even the first seven years are spent in pastime, and God looks not much at it."[7] Probably most children were set to some kind of useful work before they reached seven. Certainly Puritan spokesmen emphasized the dangers of idleness more than the permissibility of play. "Idleness in youth," said John Norton, "is scarcely healed without a scar in age. Life is but short; and our lesson is longer than admits the loss of so great an opportunity, without a sensible defect afterward shewing it self."[8] Benjamin Wadsworth admitted that "time for lawful Recre-

[4] *Essex Court Records*, II, 247; V, 311.

[5] Wadsworth, *Well-Ordered Family*, p. 50.

[6] *Massachusetts Laws of 1648*, p. 11. Cf. George Brinley, ed., *The Laws of Connecticut: An Exact Reprint of the Original Edition of 1673* (Hartford, 1858, hereafter *Connecticut Laws of 1673*), p. 13.

[7] John Cotton, *Practical Commentary upon John*, p. 124.

[8] John Norton, *Abel Being Dead yet Speaketh* (London, 1658), p. 9.

ation now and then, is not altogether to be denied them. . . . Yet for such to do little or nothing else but play in the streets, especially when almost able to earn their living is a great sin and shame."[9] Samuel Sewall, following this kind of advice, took care that his children should have more to do than play in the streets. In a letter to Daniel Allen, on March 28, 1687, he wrote: "I have two small daughters who begin to goe to schoole: my wife would intreat your good Lady to pleasure her so far as to buy for her, white Fustian drawn, enough for curtins, wallen counterpaine for a bed, and half a duz. chairs, with four threeded green worsted to work it."[10] The young seamstresses whom Sewall expected to ply the green worsted through so much fustian and counterpain were Elizabeth and Hannah Sewall, aged five and seven years respectively. That he intended the materials for them is shown by his request on the same date to his London financial agent, Edward Hull, "to furnish my Cousin Allen with what mony she calls for towards a piece of service my wife Intreat her help in, that so she may set her two Little daughters on work and keep them out of Idlenes."[11]

The daughters of a family could begin the study of a calling at such an early age, because there was little likelihood of their ever following any career but that of a housewife, whether as daughter, wife, or mother. Boys did not ordinarily undertake training in a life's occupation until they had reached a riper age. If the boy was to follow his father's calling, he might begin to pick up the rudiments of it while still very young; but in large families with children of varying talents, not all would be willing or qualified to follow their father's trade. In most cases probably one son inherited the father's business while the others took up some different occupation. They could not begin to learn it until they had decided what it should be, but they were doubtless kept busy about the house with chores of a general nature.

[9] Wadsworth, *Well-Ordered Family*, p. 47.
[10] Samuel Sewall, "Letter-Book," Massachusetts Historical Society *Collections*, sixth series, I and II; I, 44.
[11] Ibid.

A boy usually chose his calling between the ages of ten and fourteen. Since the training for almost every trade was gained through an apprenticeship of seven years to some master of the trade, if a child wished to be free and able to earn his living by the time he became twenty-one, he had to begin his apprenticeship not later than his fourteenth year. If he began it before then, as many children did, he usually remained an apprentice until he reached twenty-one.[12] Of course if he was so fortunate as to go to college, he might put off the choice of a calling until later; for the mere fact of possessing a college degree narrowed the choice: anyone with a "liberal" education would adopt a "liberal" calling, that is, a calling which required no manual labor and no long period of apprenticeship. About half the graduates of Harvard College in the seventeenth century entered the ministry.[13] Thus for many boys the decision to go to college must have constituted in itself the choice of a calling. In any case most persons had to decide their vocation in life at a comparatively early age, for unless a man underwent the long training necessary either for a liberal education or for a skilled trade, he could look forward to spending his life in a position of servitude as a common laborer.

The importance of making a good choice was heightened by the difficulties involved in changing one's mind later. After a man had gone through seven years of preparation for an occupation, he would not lightly undertake to learn another. The petition of a Boston brewer, whose license the authorities had threatened to revoke, shows the predicament of a man who was forbidden to exercise the calling in which he had been trained. The petition, dated Jan. 27, 1653/4, states that Clement Grosse "hath all his life tyme beene bred up a Brewer and knoweth not in any other lawfull calling how to ymploy himself to gett an honest liveing to mayntaine himself his wyfe and famyly." The petition of Philip Nelson, dated May

---

[12] There was no attempt in New England, as there was in old England, to set the age at twenty-four.

[13] Samuel E. Morison, *Harvard College in the Seventeenth Century*, pp. 556–563.

26, 1656, reveals a similar situation. The petitioner sought to retain the title of his father's lands for his brother and himself, because "it is the onely way (under God) and means of subsistence for the two elder sons here in New england, both being of years to follow husbandry, and not capable of any other course of life."[14] After a boy had chosen his calling, then, he seldom had an opportunity to change it. That fact gave to his decision a gravity that augmented the religious significance which Puritans attached to the word "calling."

They used the word in three senses, in each of which it retained the connotations of the transitive verb from which it originated. It always implied that someone called and that someone else was called. The subject in all three senses was God, the object always man. In the first and broadest sense God called a man to every right action that he did. If the Puritan felt justified in a given act, he perceived a calling or a call to it. If he doubted that he should do something, he said that he felt no call to it. Thus Lucy Downing wrote John Winthrop that she doubted whether her son had a call to undertake a voyage to the West Indies: "I pray pardon my earnestnes about my chilldren; for the voyage is like to be longe, the seas I aprehend more than ordinarily daungerous, and the companye as far as I hear none of the best. yet if I maye see theer calls cleare I hope [I] shall the better yeallde them, but if anny cross providences should befall them and theer way not clear, that would be a double affliction."[15] Similarly, after Thomas Shepard had narrowly escaped death by embarking for New England when it was "late in the yeare and very dangerous to goe to sea," he wrote in his autobiography that he "learnt from that time never to goe about a sad businesse in the darke, unless gods call within as well as that without be very strong and cleare and comfortable."[16]

In its second sense the word applied to the process of salvation:

---

[14] Both petitions were found in the photostat collection of the Massachusetts Historical Society (arranged by date).

[15] *Winthrop Papers*, V, 297.

[16] Colonial Society of Masssachusetts *Publications*, XXVII, pp. 377–378.

God "called" men to salvation. "The substance of this call, or the thing the Lord calls unto, is to come unto him."[17] The process was usually designated as the "general" or "effectual" calling. Thomas Hooker entitled one of his books *The Soul's Vocation or Effectual Calling*.[18]

In its last sense, distinguished as "personal" or "particular" calling, the word signified the occupation by which a man earned his living. Before the sixteenth century the usual term had been "estate"; the word "calling" had been reserved for the life of prayer and fasting to which the Lord called monks and nuns. Only those who had renounced this world were thought to serve their maker. Martin Luther, in his defiance of monasticism, declared that almost every way of life except that of monk or nun was serviceable to God and that every honest layman was called by God to his particular activity in society, whether it was making shoes or ruling the state. The cobbler, the cartwright, and the cooper could each serve God better than could the monk in his sterile seclusion.[19] From this application the word has come in common usage to mean simply the everyday occupation of a man. So it has hitherto been used in this essay. Hereafter it will be employed only in the sense of a call from God, a call which sanctified the activities to which it was applied. This was the sense in which the Puritans normally used it.[20] Every Christian, they thought, was obliged to perform the work of his particular calling "as the work of Christ." "Seeing yourself thus working in worldly employments for him [Christ]," said Thomas Shepard, "you may easily apprehend that for that time God calls you to them, and you attend upon the work of Jesus Christ in them, that you honor God as much, nay, more, by the meanest servile

---

[17] Thomas Shepard, *Works*, I, 221.

[18] London, 1637.

[19] See Ruth Mohl, *The Three Estates in Medieval and Renaissance Literature* (New York, 1933), and Ernst Troeltsch, *The Social Teaching of the Christian Churches*, tr. Olive Wyon. (New York, 1931).

[20] I say "normally," because even the Puritans sometimes used the word in the modern sense of occupation: they sometimes spoke of a "lawful calling," a phrase which would have been redundant in their ordinary use of the word.

worldly act, than if you should have spent all that time in meditation, prayer, or any other spiritual employment, to which you had
no call at that time."[21] Apart from sleep and lawful recreation a
true Christian spent his whole life in the performance of his "particular" and his "general" callings. The industrious Increase Mather
wrote in his diary, "I am not willing to allow my self above Seven
Hours in Four and Twenty, for Sleep: but would spend the rest of
my Time in Attending to the Duties of my personal or general Calling."[22] By thus yoking together in name the business of earning a
living and the duties of religion the Puritans emphasized the sacred-
ness of every man's work in the world.

The choice of a calling therefore was a solemn affair. It was not
so much a choice as a discerning of what occupation God called one
to, for since the days of immediate revelation had passed, God did
not call directly by an inward voice. He called only by general rules
which he left the individual to apply. The first rule was that no occupation served him which did not serve society. The Puritan divines made it clear that in the choice of a calling "we may not onely
aime at our own, but at the publike good,"[23] that no occupation "is
lawful but what is *useful* unto humane society."[24] On this basis the
Puritans condemned the running of private lotteries, for "tho this
or that particular man may be a *gainer,* yet it would puzzle any
man to tell what necessary or convenient *uses* of humane society,
where the lottery is opened, are at all served."[25] On this ground
also they condemned monasticism because monks served no purpose useful to society. Fasting and prayer were the duty of all
Christians by their "general" calling and did not constitute in themselves a "particular" calling.[26] "Besides, to doe as much in a generall way of charity, as that which amounts to the work of a par-

[21] Shepard, *Works,* I, 308.
[22] Quoted in Cotton Mather, *Parentator,* p. 38.
[23] John Cotton, *The Way of Life,* p. 439.
[24] This was the judgment of a meeting of ministers at Boston in 1699. Cotton
Mather, *Magnalia Christi Americana,* II, 270.
[25] Ibid.
[26] William Perkins, *Workes* (London, 1612), I, 755.

ticular calling, is *to confound generall and particular callings,* which God, and rule have distinguished."[27]

The second rule was that God called a man to a particular occupation by giving him talents and inclination for it. "When God hath called me to a place," said John Cotton, "he hath given me some gifts fit for that place."[28] Samuel Willard told the members of the Old South Church that "God doth never Call any to service but he fitts them for it, hence we have a rule to judge of our calling."[29] When Josiah Cotton, after graduating from Harvard, sought the advice of his brother John about the selection of a calling, John replied: "You must first resolve with yourself what Calling you design to follow, and to serve God and your Generation in, drawing up your conclusions from your own inclinations, and qualifications. I perceive two stand candidates with you, the practise of Physick and Theology. I believe herein it is good to indulge your Genius."[30] As a matter of fact Josiah chose neither. He decided that he lacked the genius for the ministry and so became first a schoolteacher and then a public clerk for the county of Plymouth. His liberal education enabled him to change his occupation without further training, but he later conjectured that "after all it is possible that some of my disappointments since have been owing to my thus diverting from the business designed me by my parents, and would therefore caution others against diverting from such business as they are brought up to and in some measure fit for."[31]

Perhaps if Josiah's parents had been living at the time when he made his first choice, they could have guided him to the occupation for which he was best fitted. Since a boy normally had to decide upon his lifework by the age of fourteen, he was seldom competent

---

[27] Thomas Hooker, *Survey of the Summe of Church Discipline,* Part I, p. 114.
[28] John Cotton, *The Way of Life,* p. 439.
[29] Boston Sermons, Oct. 12, 1679.
[30] Curwin Papers (manuscripts in the library of the American Antiquarian Society at Worcester, Massachusetts), III, 60 (Oct. 25, 1699). This was the grandson of the John Cotton referred to in note 28.
[31] Josiah Cotton's Memoirs (manuscript in the library of the Massachusetts Historical Society), p. 113.

to make the decision by himself. He could not understand where his best abilities lay nor could he be trusted to choose an occupation useful to society. It was therefore incumbent upon his parents to guide his choice. Their guidance must in many cases have amounted to an absolute determination. Hugh Hall's father, for instance, seems to have led him into a mercantile career against his wishes. While attending Harvard College Hugh was apparently encouraged by Benjamin Colman and John Leverett to think of himself as a candidate for the ministry. Upon returning home to Barbados he found that his father had different plans for him, and in spite of his inclinations toward the ministry he yielded to his father's superior judgment. The father wrote to Colman and Leverett explaining the situation, and Hugh meekly followed with two letters of his own:

[to Colman] I perceive by my Father, he has now Given you his Reasons for Fixing me in a Mercantile way, and fully Answered the many Weighty Arguments You were pleased to lay before him, to Induce his Permission of my Entering on a Pastoral Function.

[to Leverett] The many Cogent Arguments You used with my Father to Countenance the Inclinations I had to a Pastoral Function I suppose he has now Answered; and Given His Reasons for fixing me in a Way of Commerce; in which I have had the highest Demonstrations of His Affection, in the large Assistances now Afforded me, and the Encouraging Offers he yet Tenders; from which I doubt not (through Divine Benediction) in some little time to Establish my self well in the World.[32]

Hugh's father may have had very good reasons for "fixing" Hugh in a mercantile way, but if he had performed his duty properly, he would have paid close attention to the boy's desires and abilities. It was imperative that a child should undertake no other occupation than that in which he could best serve the Lord. If he made a false start, it was better that he try again in another direction, despite the handicaps involved, rather than go on in a work to which God

[32] Hugh Hall, Letterbook (manuscript in the Harvard College Library), pp. 8–9.

had obviously given him no call. Samuel Sewall's eldest son, Sam, changed masters twice before he found his calling, and Sewall directed him in the whole matter with paternal sympathy and anxiety. The boy was first apprenticed to a shopkeeper by the name of Perry, but in January 1695 he seems to have returned home. Thereafter for a year his father prayed constantly for "Samuel to be disposed to such a Master and Calling, as wherein he may abide with God." Sometime during the year Sam tried working with another merchant, Captain Checkly, but it now became evident that he had neither inclination nor ability for ordinary commercial transactions; he really wanted to be a bookseller. On Saturday, February 9, when he had come home for the weekend, Sewall wrote:

Last night Sam. could not sleep because of my Brother's speaking to him of removing to some other place, mentioning Mr. Usher's. I put him to get up a little wood, and he even fainted, at which Brother was much startled, and advis'd to remove him forthwith and place him somewhere else, or send him to Salem and he would doe the best he could for him. Since, I have express'd doubtfullness to Sam, as to his staying there.

He mention'd to me Mr. Wadsworth's Sermon against Idleness, which was an Affliction to him. He said his was an idle Calling, and that he did more at home than there, take one day with another. And he mention'd Mr. Stoddard's words to me, that should place him with a good Master, and where had fullness of Imployment. It seems Sam. overheard him, and now alleged these words against his being where he was because of his idleness. Mention'd also the difficulty of the imployment by reason of the numerousness of Goods and hard to distinguish them, many not being marked; whereas Books, the price of them was set down, and so could sell them readily. I spake to Capt. Checkly again and again, and he gave me no encouragement that his being there would be to Sam's profit; and Mrs. Checkly always discouraging.

Mr. Willard's Sermon from those Words, What doest thou here Elijah? was an Occasion to hasten the Removal.

Feb. 10. Secund-day. I went to Mr. Willard to ask whether had best keep him at home to day. He said, No: but tell Capt. Checkly first; but when I came back, Sam was weeping and much discompos'd and loth to goe because it was a little later than usual, so I thought twas hardly fit for him to go in that Case, and went to Capt. Checkly and told him how it was, and thank'd him for his kindness to Sam. Capt. Checkly desired Sam. might come to their house and not be strange there, for which I thank'd him very kindly. He presented his Service to my wife, and I to his who was in her Chamber. Capt. Checkly gave me Sam's Copy-book that lay in a drawer.

Just before I got thether, I met Mr. Grafford who told me that Mumford said I was a knave. The good Lord give me Truth in the inward parts, and finally give Rest unto my dear Son, and put him into some Calling wherein He will accept of him to Serve Him.

A week later Sewall wrote in his diary, "I was very sorrowfull by reason of the unsettledness of my Samuel"; and on February 26, 1695/6, he "pray'd with Sam. alone that God would direct our way as to a Calling for him." Finally the boy was able to convince his father that he could serve the Lord best by selling books, and on April 8, 1697, Sewall made an agreement with Mr. Wilkins, the bookseller, "about Sam's living with him."[33]

When a child became an apprentice, he went to live with his master and could not "absent himself day nor night from his Masters service without his leave."[34] If his parents lived in the same town as his master, he was doubtless able to visit them frequently, especially on Sundays, but I have seen only one contract which specifically provided that he be allowed to do so.[35] Moreover the court records show that a master could recover damages from overfond parents who detained their child from his work.[36] The

[33] Samuel Sewall, "Diary," I, 397, 398, 421, 422, 423, 452.

[34] From a model form for the contract of apprenticeship given in H. B., *Boston Almanack for the Year of our Lord God 1692* (Boston, 1692), in the pages at the back.

[35] *Essex Court Records*, IV, 218–220.

[36] See *Chandler* v. *Tyler*, in *Essex Court Records*, II, 403; *Buckley* v. *Quilter*, in *Essex Court Records*, II, 275; *Sevenson* v. *Remington*, in Middlesex files, Folder 45, group 2.

removal of a child from his parents when he was only fourteen years old or less seems a little strange, in view of the importance which the Puritans attached to family relations. The mere force of custom must have been partly responsible: apprenticeship was the only known way of learning a trade, and since the Middle Ages it had been customary for an apprentice to live with his master, even if his own home stood next door.[37] Yet something more than custom must have been behind the practice, for Puritan children were frequently brought up in other families than their own even when there was no apparent educational advantage involved. Not only were boys put out to learn a trade, but girls were put out to learn housekeeping. Lawrence Hammond recorded in his diary for April 23, 1688:

This day came into our family Elizabeth Nevenson, daughter of Mr. John Nevinson and Elizabeth his wife, who wilbe 13 yeares of age the 22d day of October next: The verbal Covenant betweene my wife and Mrs. Nevenson is, that she the said Elizabeth shall dwell with my wife as a servant six yeares, to be taught, instructed and provided for as shalbe meet, and that she shall not depart from our family during the said time without my wives consent.[38]

It might be argued that Elizabeth Nevenson's parents were too poor to maintain their daughter themselves and therefore made her a servant to Mrs. Hammond; but the designation of her father as "Mr." John Nevenson belies that explanation: the title "Mister" or "Master" was reserved in the seventeenth century for persons of wealth and social distinction. What her parents gained by making her a servant is not clear. Nor is it clear why Samuel Fuller of Plymouth took into his family three children not his own while he sent his daughter to live in another family. He certainly could not have gained financially, since he had to pay for the keep of his daughter: his will, dated July 30, 1633, provided that "my daughter *Mercy* be and remain to goodwife *Wallen* so long as she will keepe

---

[37] See Robert F. Seybolt, *Apprenticeship and Apprenticeship Education in Colonial New England and New York* (New York, 1917), p. 13.
[38] Massachusetts Historical Society *Proceedings*, XXVII, 146.

her at a reasonable charge."[39] Children left the parental roof not only to live with the masters to whom they were apprenticed, but frequently to live with their schoolmaster. Sewall's granddaughter attended boarding school in Boston at the age of nine.[40] Moreover, children made long visits in the homes of friends, and not always at their own desire. Sewall recorded in October 1693 that he took his own daughter, then aged thirteen, to live with a family in Rowley and that when he rode home, he had "much adoe to pacify my dear daughter, she weeping and pleading to go with me."[41] Sewall gave no hint as to why she should not have gone with him. Neither he nor any other New England writer indicated the purpose of these economically unnecessary removals of children from home, but almost every surviving correspondence of seventeenth-century New England gives evidence that the custom existed.

In explanation I suggest that Puritan parents did not trust themselves with their own children, that they were afraid of spoiling them by too great affection. The custom of placing children in other families already existed in England in the sixteenth century. Foreigners visiting the country attributed it to lack of parental affection, but Englishmen justified it on the grounds that a child learned better manners when he was brought up in another home than his own.[42] The Puritans in continuing the practice probably had the same end in view. Certainly some parents were not fit to bring up their own children, for the ministers took notice that many fathers and mothers "seem to make Conscience not to Expect or Challeng it [honor and reverence] from their Children, either in *Word* or *Gesture,* being ready to account it a Sin so to do; as that which Christian Parents *Ought not,* or at least *Need not* be concerned about."[43] When parents took this attitude, children became overfamiliar, "as if hail-fellow well met (as they say) and no difference

---

[39] *New England Historical and Genealogical Register*, IV, 33.

[40] Sewall, "Letter-Book," II, 108–109.

[41] Sewall, "Diary," I, 385.

[42] Lewis Einstein, *Tudor Ideals* (New York, 1921), pp. 245–246.

[43] Deodat Lawson, *The Duty and Property of a Religious Housholder* (Boston, 1693), p. 51.

twixt parent and child"; there were too many children, the ministers said, "who carry it proudly, disdainfully and scornfully towards parents."[44]

Such conduct was inexcusable, for by the laws of God an incorrigibly disobedient child deserved death. New England laws provided that punishment for a rebellious son and for any child who should smite or curse his parents;[45] but rather than apply this extreme penalty, the courts directed another law against parents whose affections blinded them to their children's faults. When children were allowed to become "rude, stubborn and unruly," the state might take them from their parents "and place them with some masters for years (boyes till they come to twenty one, and girls eighteen years of age compleat) which will more strictly look unto, and force them to submit unto government . . . if by fair means and former instructions they will not be drawn unto it."[46] Under the terms of this law the state compelled some parents to do what others did voluntarily. When Sarah Gibbs behaved "very sinfully and disorderly," the Court ordered "that Shee should bee put to service."[47]

Psychologically this separation of parents and children may have had a sound foundation. The child left home just at the time when parental discipline causes increasing friction, just at the time when a child begins to assert his independence. By allowing a strange master to take over the disciplinary function, the parent could meet the child upon a plane of affection and friendliness. At the same time the child would be taught good behavior by someone who would not forgive him any mischief out of affection for his person.

When a parent had safely brought his offspring through infancy and childhood and had disposed them in families where they might

[44] Thomas Cobbett, *A Frutifull and Usefull Discourse touching the Honour due from Children to Parents and the Duty of Parents towards their Children* (London, 1656), p. 94.
[45] *Massachusetts Laws of 1648*, p. 6; *Connecticut Laws of 1673*, pp. 9–10.
[46] *Massachusetts Laws of 1648*, p. 11; *Connecticut Laws of 1673*, pp. 13–14.
[47] "Records of the Particular Court of Connecticut," in Connecticut Historical Society *Collections*, XXII, 97

learn suitable occupations, he had to take one more step for their material welfare. Through skill in their callings they gained an independent economic existence, but in order to set up independent households they needed husbands and wives. Parents had not fulfilled their obligations until they saw *"their Children well dispos'd of, well settled in the World,"*[48] that is, well married and established in homes of their own; nor could a parent fulfill this duty if his children made their matches without his consent, for children would be only too apt to marry out of some vain affection, without attention to reason or religion. Parental wisdom was to be trusted in the business of choosing a mate, as in that of discerning a calling. Of course parents did not undertake to win a sweetheart for their son—but they frequently determined what lady he should address, and they almost always determined what young man should be given the chance to court their daughter. The laws of New England provided that no one should "draw away the Affections of any Maid within this Jurisdiction under pretence of Marriage, before he hath obtained liberty and allowance from her Parents or Governours."[49]

Young men who omitted this preliminary found that it was no mere formality: the court records show that many were punished for neglecting it.[50] A parent might be rather particular about the person to whom he granted access to his daughter. Sewall, for example, showed himself distinctly cool to the application of Colonel William Dudley:

[Sept. 26, 1719] Col. Wm. Dudley calls, and after other discourse, ask'd me [leave?] to wait on my daughter Judith home, when 'twas fit for her to come; I answered, It was reported he had applyed to her and he said nothing to me, when rode with me to Dedham. As came back, I call'd at his house as I had said, and he

---

[48] Wadsworth, *Well-Ordered Family*, p. 58.

[49] *Massachusetts Laws of 1648*, p. 12. See also *Connecticut Laws of 1673*, p. 46; *Plymouth Records*, XI, 190.

[50] See, for example, *Essex Court Records*, I, 180, 287; II, 242, and "Records of the Particular Court of Connecticut," in Connecticut Historical Society *Collections*, XXII, 31, 33, 51, 124, 138.

was not at home. His waiting on her might give some Umbrage:

[Oct. 13, 1719] Governor Dudley visits me in his Chariot; speaks to me in behalf of Col. Wm. Dudley, that I would give him leave that he might visit my daughter Judith. I said 'twas a weighty matter. I would consider of it &c.[51]

Sewall may have been prejudiced against Dudley, for he had already encountered bad luck in marrying his son to another member of the Dudley family. Apart from personal bias, however, the usual factors affecting parental consent for a marriage were two, religion and wealth. The ministers, of course, consistently urged that religion should outbalance wealth. Benjamin Wadsworth said that "Vertue and Piety are rather to be sought for, in an Husband or Wife, than Beauty or Riches";[52] and Increase Mather exhorted parents to "Look at Religion and the fear of God in the Disposal of your Children, That blessed man Mr. *Dod* (the Moses of his time) would sometimes bewail it, that Professours of Religion would say, *There is a* Portion *and* Civility, *and we will hope for Grace; but* (said he) *rather make sure of Grace, and hope for Riches.*"[53] Mr. Dod's lamentations were doubtless well founded, but religion did nevertheless influence parental decisions. Emmanuel Downing, for example, feared to lose his good reputation by marrying his daughter to an unregenerate but wealthy suitor. He wrote to John Winthrop:

SIR,—According your direction I have advised with mr. Endicott and some others about mr. Pester with whom I am rather encouradged to proceede then to breake of, but mr. Hathorne tells me from the Elders of the Bay that yt wilbe a scandall to marry my daughter to such a man that hath noe religion he sayth that I was stayned in poynt of coveteousnes in mr. Cooks buisines, for demaunding my monie before yt was dew; (wherein mr. Sheapheard having the papers I sent may doe me right.) And now in this

[51] Sewall, "Diary," III, 229, 231.
[52] Wadsworth, *Well-Ordered Family*, p. 43.
[53] Increase Mather, "A Discourse concerning the Danger of Apostacy," in *A Call from Heaven* (Boston, 1685), p. 128.

match, yt wilbe confirmed in theire opinions that I prefere the world
above all, which is farr contrarie to my desire and resolution,

Its well knowne how my daughter hath lost fayre opportunityes,
and in those tymes when I had monie at will, to have spared hir,
whereof shee is now verie sensible, and feares that if shee should
refuse Mr. Pester shee may stay long ere shee meet with a better,
unles I had more monie for hir then now I can spare. I pray afoard
me your Councell herein.[54]

The records indicate that Mr. Pester was rejected, but there can be
no doubt that his wealth carried great weight, for every parent, by
instinct as well as by duty, wished to see his child start married life
under advantageous material conditions. It was taken for granted,
as Downing had previously told John Winthrop, Jr., that "noe man
. . . will parte with his child till he know how shee shall be provided
for to live in the world."[55] When Wait Winthrop sought his brother's advice about a proposed match for his daughter, Fitz-John
wrote:

I am wholy unacquainted both what imployment he proposes for
a livelyhood and what estate his father proposes to settle on him;
and unlesse somthing considerable be proposed to be settled on her
in case he should dye before her, or other accident hapen, I cannot
advise you to dispose of her. She is well now; but if a woman be left
with nobody knows how many smale children, she had need have
somthing to trust too.[56]

As these statements suggest, the arrangement of a match was
contingent upon satisfying a girl's parents that she would be well
taken care of. It was pointed out in the previous chapter that a
boy's parents might also withhold their approval if the girl's dowry
were not large enough. Since their own children stood to gain, it
might be supposed that parents would have vied with each other
to see who should give the proposed couple more. Instead they
bickered and bargained and parted reluctantly with every penny

[54] *Winthrop Papers*, IV, 502.
[55] *Winthrop Papers*, III, 194–195.
[56] Massachusetts Historical Society *Collections*, fifth series, VIII, 491.

above their preconceived notion of a sufficient settlement. When Simon Bradstreet was arranging the marriage of his daughter to the son of Jonathan Wade of Ipswich, Wade offered to give his son half of his farm at Mystic and to will him a third of his land in England. Bradstreet held out for a deed of gift of the land in England. After they had parted with the matter undecided, it became apparent that Wade would not give in and so Bradstreet "consented to accept of what hee had formerly ingaged, and left it to him to add what he pleased towards the building of him a house &c., and soe agreed that the yong persons might proceede in marriage with both our consents which accordingly they did."[57] Sewall recorded some similar bargaining on the occasion of his daughter's marriage to Joseph Gerrish: "Dine with Mr. Gerrish, son Gerrish, Mrs. Anne. Discourse with the Father about my Daughter Mary's Portion. I stood for making £550 doe: because now twas in six parts, the Land was not worth so much. He urg'd for £600. at last would split the £50. Finally Febr. 20. I agreed to charge the House-Rent, and Difference of Money, and make it up £600."[58] The bickering might have gone on forever had there not been a yardstick by which the justice of a settlement could be approximately measured. There is some evidence that the normal ratio was for the girl's parents to give half as much as the boy's. For example, when William Dodge and John Procter were arranging a match between their children, Dodge engaged to give his son a tract of land while Procter promised £40 with his daughter. Dodge then asked, "Notwithstanding what is Given: what shall thess young beginers do for housshould stuff?" and at the suggestion of a third party Procter agreed to give £5 more and Dodge £10.[59] In another case Hugh March promised to give his son £132 if Joseph Fletcher gave his daughter £66.[60]

When the bargaining had been satisfactorily completed, the fi-

---

[57] *New England Historical and Genealogical Register*, XIII, 204.
[58] Sewall, "Diary," II, 336.
[59] *Essex Court Records*, V, 195.
[60] *Essex Court Records*, VIII, 244.

nancial agreement was drawn up in a legal contract and consent to
the marriage given. The parent's responsibility for his child would
normally end here. But even after the marriage had taken place, it
was the parents who filed suit and carried on the litigation when the
financial agreements were not fulfilled. Thus when Hugh March
failed to deliver the £132 he had promised to his son upon marriage
with Joseph Fletcher's daughter, it was Fletcher who brought the
matter to court.[61] A similar situation occurred in a contest over the
will of John Endicott. When Endicott died, he left with his son a
paper which confirmed that "I the said John Endecott Governour
Gave unto my Eldest sonn John Endecott upon contract of marriage, with Elizabeth the daughter of mr. Jeremiah Houchen of
Bostone, within the Jurisdiction aforesaid All and every part of
that my farme, with all the houses and appurtenances whatsoever,
which I had and purchased of Henry H Chickering of Dedham in
the County of Suffolk."[62] In the will which accompanied this paper,
Endicott left his "Orchard Farm" to his widow. Jeremiah Houchen
thereupon contested the will upon the ground that Endicott had
promised the Orchard Farm as well as the Chickering Farm to his
son at the time that the latter married Houchen's daughter, "wheer
uppon this deponant gave his daughter to wife unto his Son and
without that thee match had neever been Consented unto: by this
deponant: and this deponant did not in thee least doubt but John
Endicott Son to thee Governour should accordingly Injoy thee
Orchard farme."[63] It was Houchen, not the son, who contested the
will. Sometimes a parent even undertook the divorce proceedings
when a match proved unsatisfactory. Mary Atkinson's father sued
for her divorce when her husband deserted her, and Mary Litchfield's mother performed the same service for her.[64]

The authority of parents in matters of marriage was great, but it
was not unlimited. They could withhold access to their daughters;

[61] Ibid.
[62] From a volume of miscellaneous manuscripts in the library of the Massachusetts Historical Society, numbered 012.4, p. 30.
[63] Colonial Society of Massachusetts *Publications*, XX, 262.
[64] See ch. II, nn. 30 and 33.

they could refuse permission for a match and thereby prevent it; they could withhold a dowry or a settlement from a disobedient child; but they could not neglect their children's wishes and still be good Puritans. They could not rightfully insist that a child marry someone whom he disliked, for the child would then be unable to fulfill the duty of loving his mate. The ministers forbade all parents "to put a force on their children," because "neither Reason nor Religion" allowed it.[65] "Having faithfully and discreetly advised their Children," the ministers continued, "they should not too Tyranically impose upon them," for "We know by long Experience that forc'd Matches any way seldome do well."[66] After Betty Sewall had rejected several suitors suggested by her father, he told her in a rather sharp letter that if she refused Mr. Hirst, it would "tend to discourage persons of worth from making their Court to you. . . . Yet notwithstanding, if you find in yourself an immovable incurable Aversion from him, and cannot love, and honour, and obey him, I shall say no more, nor give you any further trouble in this matter. It had better be off than on."[67]

Betty married Mr. Hirst. Like many other dutiful Puritan children, she seems to have remained wholly subject to her parents' wishes, except to reject the suitors whom she felt that she could never love. The children of John Winthrop, Jr., showed themselves equally amenable to parental guidance. When Winthrop had arranged a match for his daughter Elizabeth, he wrote to his son Fitz-John: "As for your sister, although hir inclination was rather that way then any other that presenteth, yet hir constant professions and resolutions have bene to doe nothing without our approbation, and so hath beene very well contented hitherto to submit to such condition as we should see providence directing us to consent to for hir future good and comfort. . . ."[68] When Fitz-John's own marriage came under consideration, he made the same profession

---

[65] Willard, *Compleat Body of Divinity*, p. 604.
[66] John Cotton, *A Meet Help*, p. 18.
[67] Sewall, "Letter-Book," I, 213.
[68] Massachusetts Historical Society *Collections*, fifth series, VIII, 48.

of obedience as his sister. In a letter to his father in 1661 he wrote:

Sir, what you shall please to direct for my waye of settlement I shall redily comply with your pleasure theirein, though if my owne inclination should have any share in the disposall of myself, I would not as yet accept the profer of a maried life . . . However, my owne will and desires shall be subordinate to your pleasure and intensions concerning me, and shall not act anything theirein without your free and willing approbation in a case of such importance.[69]

Such statements might justify the assumption that Puritan children were entirely passive in the choice of their husbands and wives except when they felt a positive aversion to the proposed spouse. Doubtless many marriages did take place in which the bride and groom were merely carrying out a parental decision, but more frequently the Puritan fathers must have confined the exercise of their power to haggling over the financial agreement after the children had chosen for themselves—provided of course that they had chosen within the proper economic and religious limitations. In 1707 Fitz-John Winthrop himself admitted that "it has been the way and custome of the country for young folkes to choose, and where there is noe visible exception everybody approves it."[70] Embarrassing results sometimes followed when children, presuming upon the consent of their parents, went ahead to make their own matches. When Michael Wigglesworth was first thinking of marriage, he offered himself to a young lady in New Haven. He had no sooner done so than he received word from his mother in Weathersfield,

declaring that they had propounded a business of the like nature there in my behalf, and that I was now engaged in a sute there, and therefore to see that issued before I look't any further. This report did fill my spirit suddenly with marvellous sorrow and perplexity more than I wel knew how to bear; insomuch that I

---

[69] Massachusetts Historical Society *Collections*, fifth series, VIII, 270.
[70] Massachusetts Historical Society *Collections*, sixth series, III, 396.

fear'd least the violence of it should overthrow my bodily health. I was affraid my withdrawing should seem contempt of the party who was of great note and birth and piety, and cast shame upon my friends who had motion'd such thing as from me.

In this trying situation Wigglesworth did what any good Puritan would have done: he prayed and then wrote letters,

endeavouring to undoe what was done. But my letters could not be sent that week. upon the last day comes news that the business was issued, and the party was to go for England and not to be dispozed of here. At this news my heart was filled with joy and enlarged to bless the Lord with my soul and all that was within me. And I desire I may never forget this answer of prayer, and this mercifull taking of my soul out of trouble.[71]

Another kind of difficulty developed when the son of William Leete captured the heart of a lady whose father had gone to England. In spite of numerous letters dispatched to the absent parent, no word could be drawn from him, so that Leete had to entreat the aid of John Winthrop, Jr., to search him out and obtain consent for the match. The young couple, said Leete, had set their affections on each other and were known to be in love "throughout the cuntry, so as it would be a thing destructive to themselves and dishonorable to us all, if Mr. Jordan should not consent."[72] In sum, it appears that parents and children had both to consent to a match and that in practice either might take the first steps to bring it about.

[71] Colonial Society of Massachusetts *Publications*, XXXV, 394.
[72] Massachusetts Historical Society *Collections*, fourth series, VII, 558.

IV

The Education
of a Saint

*A*S FAR as his children's material welfare was concerned, a
Puritan parent could call his duty done when he saw them established in their callings with good husbands and wives. But he was
responsible for the well-being of their souls as well as their bodies.
If he considered only their material welfare without attention to
their spiritual needs, he was, the Puritans thought, like those "who
are very careful for the shooe, and take no care for the foot."[1] He
lacked common sense. He also lacked religion. Cotton Mather
pointed out to the earnest inhabitants of Boston that "If your *main
concern* be, to get the *Riches* of *this World* for your *Children,* and
leave a *Belly full* of this *World* unto them, it looks very suspi-
ciously, as if you were yourselves the People of *this World,* whose
Portion is only in *this Life.*"[2] The point was a telling one, but the
Puritans did not rely on mere exhortation to persuade parents of
their spiritual duties. In 1642 Massachusetts enacted a law requiring masters of families to teach their children and apprentices to
read. As amplified six years later, the law required that no one
should

suffer so much barbarism in any of their families as not to indeavour to teach by themselves or others, their children and

---

[1] John Norton, *Abel Being Dead yet Speaketh,* p. 7.
[2] Cotton Mather, "What the Pious Parent Wishes," in *A Course of Sermons
on Early Piety* (Boston, 1721), p. 9.

apprentices so much learning as may inable them perfectly to read the english tongue, and knowledge of the Capital lawes: upon penaltie of twentie shillings for each neglect therin. Also that all masters of families doe once a week (at the least) catechize their children and servants in the grounds and principles of Religion, and if any be unable to doe so much: that then at the least they procure such children or apprentices to learn some short orthodox catechism without book, that they may be able to answer unto the questions that shall be propounded to them out of such catechism by their parents or masters or any of the Select men when they shall call them to a tryall of what they have learned in this kinde.[3]

The grounds of the law are clear: the Puritans insisted upon education in order to insure the religious welfare of their children. This motive certainly explains the requirement that children learn a catechism. It also explains in large measure why they should know the capital laws, for the capital laws were simply the most important of the laws of God, an understanding of which was essential to the welfare of the smallest child. In the printed codes of law, the capital laws alone had the distinction of being supported by biblical citation. It might be contended that the reading requirement arose from a pure love of knowledge in itself, but the reasons which the Puritans offered elsewhere in defense of reading make it plain that here again a religious motive was present. In 1647 the General Court of Massachusetts provided for the establishment of reading schools, because it was *one chief project of that old deluder, Satan, to keep men from the knowledge of the Scriptures.*[4] Children were taught to read in order that they might gain a first-hand knowledge of the Bible. When John Cotton was urging parents to educate their children, he did not say, "Learn them to read," but "Learn them to read the Scriptures."[5] Benjamin Wadsworth ex-

---

[3] *Massachusetts Laws of 1648*, p. 11; M. W. Jernegan, *Laboring and Dependent Classes in Colonial America, 1607–1783.* (Chicago, 1931), pp. 84–99.
[4] *Massachusetts Laws of 1648*, p. 47. On the development of New England schools prior to 1647, see Jernegan, *Laboring and Dependent Classes*, pp. 69–83.
[5] John Cotton, *Practical Commentary upon John*, p. 102.

horted young persons to the same purpose. "If we are not able to *Read,* we should use all regular means, and imploy all opportunities for our learning; but if we can *read,* we should not (unless some extraordinary matter prevents) suffer one day to pass, without reading some portion of the Word of God."[6] Thomas Foxcroft was even more explicit in his explanation of the need for education:

The Word Written and Preacht is the ordinary Medium of Conversion and Sanctification. Now in order to obtaining these Benefits by the Word, it is requisite, that Persons be diligent in *Reading and Hearing* of it; And in order to these, how expedient and necessary is it, that there be Schools of Learning; those of a Lower Character, for the instructing of Youth in Reading, and those of an Higher, for the more Liberal Education of such, as may be devoted to the Work of the Ministry?[7]

The Puritans sought knowledge, therefore, not simply as a polite accomplishment, nor as a means of advancing material welfare, but because salvation was impossible without it. They retained throughout the seventeenth century a sublime confidence that man's chief enemy was ignorance, especially ignorance of the Scriptures. By keeping the world in ignorance, they thought, the Roman Church had stifled true religion. When the people finally recovered knowledge of the Scriptures, the light of the gospel broke out in the Reformation, and as long as the people had this knowledge, the light would continue to shine. The Puritans rested their whole system upon the belief that "Every *Grace* enters into the Soul through the *Understanding.*"[8] Upon this premise it followed naturally that "The *Devotion* of *Ignorance,* is but a *Bastard* sort of *Devotion,*" or that "Ignorance is the Mother (not of Devotion but) of HERESY."[9] In order to be saved, men had to understand the doctrines of Christianity, and since children were born without

[6] Benjamin Wadsworth, *Exhortations to Early Piety* (Boston, 1702), p. 51.
[7] Thomas Foxcroft, *Cleansing Our Way in Youth* (Boston, 1719), p. 176.
[8] Cotton Mather, *Cares about the Nurseries* (Boston, 1702), p. 34.
[9] Ibid., and Increase Mather, "A Discourse concerning the Danger of Apostacy," in *A Call from Heaven*, p. 127.

understanding, they had to be taught. Samuel Willard, in a sermon to the members of the Old South Church, explained the dangers to which all children were exposed by their ignorance. John Hull copied down the minister's words as follows:

1. they are all born in Ignorance rom. 3.17. without the knowledge and fear of god they must have it by doctrine and institution 2ly this ignorance layeth them open to satan to lead them whither he will. 3ly holdeth them under the Power [and] efficacy of sin a blind mind and dead conscience are companions. hence they sin without shame ignorance stopps the activity of all the faculties. 4ly as long as they remain in their naturall ignorance there is no hope of being freed from everlasting misery. if you have any Compassion for them take Pains that they may know god. 5ly Hardness of heart allienation from god Springs from ignorance and 6ly they hence are inclined to fullfill their owne evill will.[10]

Such doctrines make it apparent that if children were not to remain forever "*Alienated from the Life of God*," parents must teach them "the *Worth* of a Christ, and their *Want* of a Christ, and a way of closing with a *Christ*." "*After* all, (nay, *Before* all, and *Above* all,)" said Cotton Mather,

Tis the *Knowledge* of the *Christian Religion,* that *Parents* are to *Teach* their *Children.* . . . The *Knowledge* of other things, though it be never so desirable an Accomplishment for them, our *Children* may arrive to Eternal Happiness without it. But the *Knowledge* of the *Godly Doctrine in the words of the Lord Jesus Christ,* is of a Million times more Necessity for them; without that *Knowledge,* our Children are Miserable to all *Eternity.*[11]

In other words, the main business of education was to prepare children for conversion by teaching them the doctrines and moral precepts of Christianity.

Parents who themselves had been converted were especially bound to educate their children. God made the "covenant of grace" with a believer and his seed: he promised godly parents that he

---

[10] Boston Sermons, August 31, 1679.
[11] Cotton Mather, *Cares about the Nurseries,* pp. 12–13, 34.

would save their children as well as themselves. As extended to children, however, the promise was not unconditional, for even a believer's children were born ignorant. The covenant did not give them an absolute claim to salvation, but it did give them a better chance than other children. If they were properly brought up, it was almost certain that the promise would be fulfilled. "Holy bringing up of children is one special meanes of conveying the blessing of the Covenant unto them,"[12] said Peter Bulkeley, and Thomas Cobbett pointed out

that the greatest love and faithfulness which Parents as Covenanters can shew to God, and to their Children, who in and with themselves, are joynt Covenanters with God, is so to educate them, that what in them lieth, the conditions of the Covenant may be attended by their Children, and so the whole Covenant fully effected, in the promised mercies of it also to them, and to their Children.[13]

In other words, children, who by their parents' covenant were half saved, might by education become wholly saved.

As far as children were concerned, the conditional promise was God's part in the covenant of grace; the believer's part was to bring up his children so that the promise might be fulfilled. The children, after all, belonged to God. "He calls them *His* . . . they belong to Him by Covenant; they have been solemnly consecrated to his Service: and what, will you not bring them up for him, to whom you have thus solemnly consecrated them?"[14] The practical certainty of the desired results must have been a powerful incentive for godly parents to educate their offspring, but if the incentive proved insufficient in any case, the ministers stood ready to remind their fellow believers that "the Children born in Our Families, are *Born unto God*, and a strict account will one day be Required of us. . . . These Children, God Committeth unto us for Education, He doth (to speak with Reverence) Put them Out to us. . . . Being

[12] Peter Bulkeley, *The Gospel-Covenant: or the Covenant of Grace opened*, 2d. edn. (London, 1651), p. 162.
[13] Cobbett, *A Fruitfull and Usefull Discourse*, p. 218.
[14] Wadsworth, *Well-Ordered Family*, p. 77.

therefore thus Committed *unto us,* Account concerning them may *Justly,* and will *Certainly,* be Required *Of us,* in the Great Day."[15] If a parent who enjoyed the covenant of grace did not enable his children also to enjoy it, he had failed to fulfill its terms and stood in danger of losing its benefits himself. If your child should "want *Knowledge,* and *Saving Wisdom* thro' any gross Negligence of thine," Cotton Mather warned, "thy punishment shall be terrible, in the Day of the Lords pleading with thee."[16] Richard Mather imagined children whose education had been neglected addressing their parents at the Day of Judgment in these words:

All this that we here suffer is through you: You should have taught us the things of God, and did not, you should have restrained us from Sin and corrected us, and you did not: You were the meanes of our Originall Corruption and guiltiness, and yet you never shewed any competent care that we might be delivered from it, from you we did receive it, by your neglect we have continued in it, and now we are damned for it: Woe unto us that we had such Carnall and careless parents, and woe unto you that had no more Compassion and pitty to prevent the everlasting misery of your own Children.[17]

The ultimate purpose of education, then, was salvation. Achievement of the purpose was complicated by the fact that children were born evil as well as ignorant. Willard's explanation of the dangers of ignorance demonstrated that uninstructed children would commit terrible sins against God because they would know no better, and he implied that these sins would be no less grievous in the sight of God because of the fact that they were committed in ignorance. Ignorance, however, did not account for an evil action but only prevented any effort to restrain it. The act itself expressed an evil nature. Willard implied as much when he said that because of ignorance children were "inclined to follow their own evil will." Anne Bradstreet made the assumption more explicit when she assigned to "Childhood" the following gloomy lines:

[15] Lawson, *The Duty and Property of a Religious Housholder,* pp. 31–32.
[16] Cotton Mather, *Corderius Americanus* (Boston, 1708), p. 14.
[17] Richard Mather, *Farewell Exhortation,* pp. 10–11.

> Stained from birth with *Adams* sinfull fact,
> Thence I began to sin as soon as act:
> A perverse will, a love to what's forbid,
> A serpents sting in pleasing face lay hid:
> A lying tongue as soon as it could speak,
> And fifth Commandment do daily break.[18]

Benjamin Wadsworth painted an even grimmer picture of child nature:

Their Hearts naturally, are a meer nest, root, fountain of Sin, and wickedness; an *evil Treasure* from whence proceed *evil things,* viz. *Evil Thoughts, Murders, Adulteries* &c. Indeed, as sharers in the guilt of *Adam's* first Sin, they're *Children of Wrath by Nature,* liable to Eternal Vengeance, the Unquencheable Flames of Hell. But besides this, their Hearts (as hath been said) are unspeakably wicked, estrang'd from God, enmity against Him, eagerly set in pursuing Vanities, on provoking God by actual Personal transgressions, whereby they merit and deserve *greater measures* of Wrath.[19]

Children would find no more encouragement in John Cotton's advice to them to "be not deluded with a good affection to your own nature you are in, this is the state of all since the world began; they are all sprauling in wickednesse, and there is such a league between the Devil and them, that unlesse the Lamb be slaughtered, we cannot be saved."[20] After she had been told such things as these, it was no wonder that little Betty Sewall burst into tears when she came to fear that she "was like Spira, not Elected."[21] The significant fact, however, is that her father wept too. Original sin was no fairy story with which to frighten little children; it was an unpleasant but inescapable fact, and the sooner children became acquainted with it, the better.

The sooner the better, because in spite of their natural wickedness children were not incorrigible. "For although there is a *Cor-*

---

[18] Anne Bradstreet, *Works*, p. 151.
[19] Benjamin Wadsworth, "The Nature of Early Piety," in *A Course of Sermons on Early Piety*, p. 10.
[20] John Cotton, *An Exposition upon the Thirteenth Chapter of the Revelation* (London, 1659), p. 199.
[21] Sewall, "Diary," I, 422.

rupt Nature in Every Child, in its Infancy . . . Yet Care and Education will much Prevail, to keep under that Corrupt Principle, and Promote better Inclinations in them."[22] For a people who believed in predestination and the absolute sovereignity of God the Puritans ascribed an extraordinary power to education. By the instruction of parents, they believed, a child could be led away from the evil to which he was naturally prone. Thus Cotton Mather wrote of his brother Nathaniel: "He wanted not the cares of his father to bestow a good *education* on him, which God blessed for the *restraining* him from the lewd and wild courses by which too many children are betimes resigned up to the possession of the devil."[23] If good habits could be instilled in a child, somehow or other, his soul would benefit. On the other hand, if he were allowed to express his evil nature habitually in evil actions, his chances of salvation would be considerably decreased. *"Use* or *custom* is a *second Nature,"* said Benjamin Wadsworth. "If we have been us'd or accustomed to a course of outward scandalous wickedness, or inward impenitency, hardness of heart, and unbelief; it will be very hard when we come to break off from it."[24] Thomas Foxcroft shared Wadsworth's view and carried its application even further. He conceived the original righteousness and subsequent corruption of man in terms of habit. With Adam's fall, he said, "the habit of Original righteousness was lost, and all moral excellencies effaced and extinguisht, and an universal permanent corruption and foul deformity introduced." By education the habit of righteousness might be partially restored, ". . . if we *accustom our selves to bear the Yoke in our Youth,* it will afterwards fit more *easy* on our Necks, it will not gall and fret us: *The Commands* will not be *grievous* unto us. Custom will lighten the Burden and endear the Yoke."[25]

The Puritans never went so far as to assert that a child could be

---

[22] Lawson, *The Duty and Property of a Religious Housholder,* p. 42.
[23] Cotton Mather, *Magnalia Christi Americana* (Hartford, 1853), II, 157.
[24] Wadsworth, *Exhortations to Early Piety,* p. 44.
[25] Foxcroft, *Cleansing Our Way,* pp. 12, 58.

saved by good habits alone. Increase Mather cautioned against such a presumption when he declared that there were many persons whose "Religion is the meer Impression of a godly Education, without any special work of the Holy Spirit upon their Souls." But he hastened to assure his listeners "that a Religious Education is a great mercy, yea, and to many of the Elect it is the great means of their Conversion."[26] Neither Mather nor any other Puritan saw a contradiction in asserting the inadequacy of education in one breath and the desirability of it in the next. Good habits did not themselves bring saving grace, but they furnished one of the main channels through which grace could flow. God alone would determine whether the channel should be filled, but when he saved a man, he often used this means. It was important to teach a child good habits, not because they would save him, but because it was unlikely that he would be saved without them. If his education was neglected, his chance of salvation was small, but if education had provided a means of grace, there was every hope that God would use the means. "Let's bring our children as neer to Heaven as we can," urged Thomas Hooker. "It is in our power to restrain them, and reform them, and that we ought to do"; for although "Restraining Grace is but common Grace, yet . . . by this means the work of Conversion is more easie."[27] Even Increase Mather attributed much of the responsibility for his conversion to the fact that his parents had restrained his evil nature: "The great Care of my Godly Parents, was to bring me up in *the Nurture and the Admonition of the Lord;* Whence I was kept from many Visible outbreakings of Sin, which else I had been Guilty of; and whence it was, that I had many good Impressions of the Spirit of GOD upon me; even from my Infancy."[28]

When education was neglected in childhood, the error could not be redeemed in age: evil nature could be trained into good habits only if the training started early. It was never too soon to begin.

---

[26] Increase Mather, *Some Important Truths About Conversion*, p. 36.
[27] Thomas Hooker, *The Application of Redemption*, p. 357.
[28] Cotton Mather, *Parentator*, p. 7.

To the question "WHEN should we *Begin* to *Teach our Children*, the *Knowledge of the Holy Scriptures?*" Cotton Mather answered "BETIMES! BETIMES! Let the Children have the *Early Knowledge* of the *Holy Scriptures*."[29] John Cotton explained why: "These Babes are flexible and easily bowed; it is far more easy to train them up to good things now, than in their youth and riper years."[30] Moreover, the ministers urged, Satan never hesitated to begin his assaults upon children in their infancy, "and therefore if you would prevent him, do not you delay, but be dropping in instruction as they are able, and as soon as they are able to understand any thing."[31] "While you lay them in your bosoms, and dandle them on your knees, try by little and little to infuse good things, holy truths into them."[32] Cotton Mather wrote of Nathaniel Rogers that the principles of religion "were instilled into his young soul with the counsels of his pious mother, while he yet sat on her knees."[33] Evidently the Puritans had no misgivings about children's abilities to assimilate knowledge. Though they were conscious of the fact that overinstruction might defeat its own ends, they never believed that instruction should wait upon years. Children were taught as fast as they could learn, and the maxim "a young saint and an old devil" was regarded as an invention of the devil. "There have been *Young Hypocrites,* that have made *Old Devils,*" said Cotton Mather, "there have been *young Sinners,* that have made *Old Divels;* but *Young Saints* will make *Old Angels;* and, blessed be God, there are such *Young Saints* in the World."[34] The ideal which Mather set before children was to be old in knowledge though young in years. "You may *Dy* in your Childhood," he advised them, "But you should be ambitious, that if it should be so, you may *dy an hundred years old;* have as much

[29] Cotton Mather, *Corderius Americanus*, p. 7.

[30] John Cotton, *Practical Commentary upon John*, p. 92.

[31] Samuel Willard, *Useful Instructions for a Professing People* (Cambridge, 1673), p. 38.

[32] Wadsworth, *Well-Ordered Family*, p. 60.

[33] Cotton Mather, *Magnalia Christi Americana*, I, 415.

[34] Cotton Mather, *Early Religion Urged*, p. 19.

Knowledge and *Vertue,* as many men of an *hundred years old.*"[35]

Children were ignorant and children were evil; but ignorance could be enlightened and evil restrained, provided the effort was made soon enough. The pious parent therefore was faced with two tasks, instruction and discipline. He had to fill his children's minds with knowledge and he had to make them apply their knowledge in right action. There was no question of developing the child's personality, of drawing out or nourishing any desirable inherent qualities which he might possess, for no child could by nature possess any desirable qualities. He had to receive all good from outside himself, from education—and ultimately from the Holy Spirit. The process of instruction was one of "infusing" or "instilling" or "dropping" the waters of knowledge into an empty receptacle. The problem of discipline was to make an evil natured but at least partly rational animal act against his nature and according to his reason.

Instruction began as soon as children were able to absorb it, but they were subjected to no intensive or formalized program at first. Peter Bulkeley pointed out that "Children whiles they are young (at which time our pious education of them must begin) are like narrow mouth'd vessels, which can receive that which is powred into them, but by drops." Therefore the best method for the first few years was to be *"Often* speaking to them of good things, now a little, and then a little, line upon line, precept upon precept, little and often, as they are able to receive."[36] Wadsworth suggested "that you should do something at it when you *lie down,* and when you *rise up,* when you *walk by the way,* and when you *set in the house,* When you are *dressing* or *undressing* your Children morning and evening."[37] Cotton Mather was always devising instructions to suit different occasions. If his children fell sick, he reminded them of "the analogous Distempers of their Souls," and instructed them "how to look up unto their great Saviour for the Cure of those Distempers." If they were playing, he observed what "Games and

[35] Cotton Mather, *Corderius Americanus*, p. 18.
[36] Bulkeley, *Gospel-Covenant*, p. 162.
[37] Wadsworth, *Well-Ordered Family*, p. 63.

Sports" they were engaged in and suggested to them "those pious Instructions, which the Circumstances of their play may lead them to think upon." He made it a rule "rarely to lett one of my Children to come anear me, and never to sitt any Time with them, without some explicit Contrivance and Endeavour, to lett fall some Sentence or other, that shall carry an useful Instruction with it."[38]

This occasional instruction could be continued even when the children grew older, but it did not exempt them from more formal tuition as soon as their minds were strong enough. Once a week at least, according to law, every father was supposed to teach his children from a catechism, a book which summarized in the form of questions and answers the Puritan system of Christian belief. Such books were available in great variety, all "design'd, as an easy, short and useful way, to instruct persons (young ones especially) in the great truths and duties of Religion."[39] Whichever one a parent chose, he would find in it "The summ of what we are to *Teach* our *Children*."[40] In order to use the book he had only to ask the questions and see whether the child could answer them without assistance. The child, of course, was supposed to study the book and learn the answers by heart.

This method of instruction was not designed to give play to the development of individual initiative, because individual initiative in religion usually meant heresy. If a child held new ideas about doctrine, they were likely to be heretical. Let him therefore memorize his catechism and leave originality to the devil. It did not follow, however, that he should simply learn the answers without making an effort to understand them. Cotton Mather cautioned parents not to let "the *Children* patter out by Rote the words of the *Catechism*, like *Parrots;* but be Inquisitive how far their *Understandings* do take in the Things of God."[41] "Instruct them," Samuel Torrey advised, "not only to say their Catechismes [but] to understand their Catechismes; and be well grounded in all the principles of

---

[38] Cotton Mather, "Diary," II, 104, 144, 150–151.
[39] Wadsworth, *Well-Ordered Family*, p. 62.
[40] Cotton Mather, *Cares about the Nurseries*, p. 15.
[41] Cotton Mather, *Cares about the Nurseries*, p. 20.

religeon; by a sound solid knowledge and beleife of them, that soe
they not forget it; and be never the better for it."[42] Children began
to learn their catechism before they could possibly know the meaning of what they said, but as they grew older, a good parent would
make them see the significance of their answers. "Tho' you should
inculcate divine things on them as soon as may be," said Benjamin
Wadsworth, "yet when they are capable of more knowledge; you
should indeavour that they may *understand the true meaning,* of
those things which are taught them."[43] Cotton Mather gave specific
instructions to assist parents in this endeavor:

And that we may be sure of it, let us *Try* and *Help* their *Understandings,* by breaking every *Answer* of the *Catechism* into little
Parcels by *Questions,* whereto YES, or NO, or one word or two,
shall be all the *Answer.* To Exemplify it. You know the *first Answer*
of that *Catechism,* which the famous Dr. *Usher* pronounced, *The
best Extant in the world,* is This; *Mans chief End is to Glorify
God, and Enjoy Him forever.* Well, when the *Child* has Recited
this, then ask him;
*What? Then is there something that every man should propound
unto himself as his chief end?*
*And, What should a man make his chief end? Only to seek him-
self, or make himself great?*
Or, to Enjoy the Riches or Pleasures of this world?
*Or, Must we propound it as our chief end to Glorify God, and
Enjoy Him forever?*
*And, if we do actively Glorify God, shall we come to Enjoy Him
forever?*
There needs but, YES or, NO, to be answered unto all these
Explanatory *Questions:* And by the YES or NO, you'l perceive
whether the *Child* have minded the Answer in the *Catechism.*

Mather continued his instructions with the suggestion that parents
should carry the doctrines into the hearts as well as the heads of
their children:

Endeavour that the *Children* may not only receive the *Catechism*

---

[42] Samuel Torrey, "Sermons at Weymouth" (manuscript in the library of the
Massachusetts Historical Society), p. 96.
[43] Wadsworth, *Well-Ordered Family,* p. 62.

into their *Understandings,* but also have their *Affections* and *Practices* conformed to what they understand . . . When we are *Catechising* our *Children,* we are *Delivering* unto them a *Form of Doctrine;* and we should contrive all the Charms imaginable, that their *Hearts* and *Lives* may be *Moulded* into that *Form.*

As now; when we Teach our *Children,* what the *Catechism* sayes, about their *Sin,* their *Original Sin,* their *Actual Sin,* and the *Wages* of their *Sin,* we may let fall some such Admonition upon them;

And, My Child, Is it not a sad thing to be a Sinner? Should not you seek above all things to be saved from your Sins?

When we Teach our *Children,* what are the *Offices,* or the *Benefits* of the Lord Jesus Christ, we may let fall some such word as this upon them;

And, Child, Would you gladly have this done for you? Or, Don't you want such a Favour as this, from the Lord Jesus Christ?

When we Teach our *Children,* what is *Forbidden* and what is *Required* in the *Commandments,* we may let fall some such word as this upon them;

And, Child, Will you beg of God, that He would preserve you from this Evil, and assist you to this Good?[44]

When these instructions were followed—and Mather's diary shows that he at least followed them—catechising may have become an effective method of religious education.[45]

Besides the occasional admonitions and weekly catechisings of his parents, the Puritan child was subjected to instruction in school and in church. Most of the training which he received at school was of a secular nature providing him tools for acquiring religious

[44] Cotton Mather, *Cares about the Nurseries,* pp. 20–21, 23–24.

[45] Cotton Mather also called upon schoolmasters to catechise their pupils (*Cares about the Nurseries,* p. 46), and the records show that the churches too sometimes had assemblies of children resembling Sunday schools, for the purpose of catechising (*Records of the First Church at Dorchester in New England, 1636–1734* [Boston, 1891], p. 67; *Report of the Record Commissioners, containing the Roxbury Land and Church Records* [Boston, 1881], vol. VI of the Boston Record Commissioners *Reports,* p. 191). Furthermore, as the education statute suggests, the selectmen of every town were expected to go occasionally from house to house and test the children's knowledge of their catechisms.

knowledge rather than knowledge itself. Before he was five years old he might be learning to read at a "Reading School" or "Dame School." After he had mastered his hornbook and speller and perhaps a first reader, like the *New England Primer,* he went on to a writing school, and thence, if he was a boy, to grammar school. Here he studied the classics. If his father was wealthy enough and he himself intelligent enough, he might next attend Harvard College to study the seven liberal arts. If he chose to, he might continue his education by the study of theology, with a view to entering the ministry, but the degree in liberal arts did not of itself qualify him as a minister. The narrowness of the catechising method was thus in a way offset by the school program.[46]

It should not be thought, however, that schooling conflicted with religion. The texts from which children learned to read and write in the elementary schools did set forth religious doctrines and Christian morality. The famous *New England Primer* taught the alphabet with such verses as "In Adams fall, we sinned all," and Cotton Mather himself composed a reader entitled *Good Lessons for Children,* which he designed so as "to have the Child improve in *Goodness* at the same time, that he improv'd in *Reading.*"[47] Mather also exercised his diligence in persuading schoolmasters as well as parents to catechise children. In establishing the study of the classics the Puritans had no intention of providing their children with tools for scepticism, nor did the students of Ezekiel Cheever's grammar school and of Harvard College display any signs of scepticism as a result of their studies. Throughout the seventeenth century New Englanders were able to look at the classics as simply other sourcebooks of the laws of nature, inferior to but not in conflict with the greatest sourcebook, the Bible. As far as they were concerned, a knowledge of the classics would

[46] See Robert F. Seybolt, *The Public Schools of Colonial Boston* (Cambridge, 1935), and Samuel E. Morison, *The Founding of Harvard College* (Cambridge, 1935) and *Harvard College in the Seventeenth Century* (Cambridge, 1937).

[47] Cotton Mather, "Diary," I, 555–556. No copy of the book is known to be extant.

heighten understanding of the doctrines which a child first encountered in a catechism.

As soon as children were old enough "so, as to be benefited
themselves and the Congregation not disturbed by 'em," they were
taken to church.[48] "Bring them to Church," said John Cotton, "and
help them to remember something, and tell them the meaning of it,
and take a little in good part, and encourage them, and that will
make them delight in it."[49] When the services had ended and the
family had returned home, the godly householder would question
the children to see how well they had paid attention to the preacher
and how much they had understood of what he had said. As far as
he was able, he would clarify the difficult points and apply the
doctrines to the children's lives. Theophilus Eaton, for example,
called his whole family together every Sunday evening, "and in an
obliging manner conferred with them about the things with which
they had been entertained in the house of God, shutting up all with
a prayer for the blessing of God upon them all."[50]

When the Puritan child had been catechised at home, taught at
school, and exhorted in church, he was doubtless well filled with
sound doctrine; but unless he behaved accordingly, he would be
none the better for it, and being of an evil nature, he was not likely
to choose the right simply because he knew it to be the right. If the
theoretical instruction was to have practical effect, parents themselves had to set the example. "Precept without Patterns will do
little good," warned Eleazar Mather; "you must lead them to
Christ by Examples as well as Counsel; you must set *your selves
first,* and speak by Lives as well as words; you must live Religion,
as well as talk Religion."[51] Parents might teach their children
"never so carefully, yet if you unteach them again by your vain
conversation before them, its little the better."[52] On the other hand,

[48] Joseph Belcher, *Two Sermons Preached in Dedham* (Boston, 1710), p. 12.
[49] John Cotton, *Practical Commentary upon John,* p. 102.
[50] Cotton Mather, *Magnalia,* I, 153.
[51] Eleazar Mather, *A Serious Exhortation to the Present and Succeeding
Generation in New England* (Cambridge, 1671), p. 20.
[52] Willard, *Useful Instructions,* p. 39.

neither doctrinal instruction nor good parental example would suffice. If children had been merely ignorant, no further measures would have been required, but inasmuch as they were evil as well, forceful restraint was also necessary. Because of the corruption they inherited from Adam, "Doctrine and Example alone are insufficient; Discipline is an essential part of the nurture of the Lord."[53]

Every parent had to decide for himself the proper method of disciplining his children. It has sometimes been assumed that the birch rod constituted the Puritans' only method of correction. It can hardly be doubted that many resorted to it, and it is safe to assume that some parents were excessively severe. Cotton Mather's epigram, "Better whipt, than Damn'd,"[54] expressed a large part of Puritan educational philosophy; and John Eliot's praise of chastisement even approached eloquence: "The gentle rod of the mother, is a very gentle thing, it will break neither bone nor skin: yet by the blessing of God with it, and upon the wise application of it: it would break the bond that bindeth up corruption in the heart."[55] Nevertheless, there is no proof that seventeenth-century parents employed the rod more freely than twentieth-century parents. When Sewall recorded the occasions of punishing his children, the offenses were much the same as those which still overtax parental patience. On Sept. 15, 1688, he "corrected" his son Sam for playing hookey and lying about it, "saying he had been at the Writing School, when he had not." On Nov. 6, 1692, he corrected Joseph, the future minister of the Old South Church, for equally grave misbehavior. Joseph had thrown "a knop of Brass and hit his Sister Betty on the forhead so as to make it bleed and swell; upon which, and for his playing at Prayer-time, and eating when Return Thanks, I whipd him pretty smartly." A modern parent would probably not be considered unduly severe for correcting his child "pretty smartly" under the same circumstances. A modern parent,

[53] John Norton, *Abel Being Dead*, p. 8.
[54] Cotton Mather, *Help for Distressed Parents* (Boston, 1695), p. 28.
[55] John Eliot, *The Harmony of the Gospels*, p. 29.

however, would not be likely to make the reflection that Sewall
made upon this occasion: "When I first went in (call'd by his
Grandmother) he sought to shadow and hide himself from me
behind the head of the Cradle: which gave me the sorrowful remembrance of Adam's carriage."[56]

Sewall, like other Puritans, saw all children as creatures of sin,
but he did not therefore conclude that a free application of the rod
was the way to bring them to righteousness. In fact, if he listened
to his religious advisers, he employed bodily punishment only as a
last resort; for the ministers who wrote and spoke on the subject
almost always counseled their readers and listeners to win children
to holiness by kindness rather than try to force them to it by severity. The aim of Puritan education was vastly different from that of
modern "progressive" education, but granted the difference in end,
the Puritan methods of discipline, as expounded by the ministers,
sound strikingly modern. The Reverend Richard Mather, who had
been subjected to a particularly harsh teacher during his boyhood
in England, is said to have exclaimed: "O that all school-masters
would learn wisdom, moderation, and equity towards their schol-
ars! and seek rather to win the hearts of children by righteous loving and courteous usage, than to alienate their minds by partiality
and undue severity." According to his grandson, Cotton Mather,
Richard put his own educational principles into practice. Becoming
a schoolmaster himself at the age of fifteen, he "carried it with such
wisdom, kindness, and grave reservation, as to be *loved* and *feared*
by his young folks, much above the most that ever used the
ferula."[57] If Cotton Mather is to be trusted, Grandfather Richard
was no exception among Puritan schoolmasters. In a funeral sermon for Ezekiel Cheever, who kept the Boston grammar school for
seventy years, Cotton expressed his assurance that the schoolmasters of New England "do watch against the *Anger which is fierce,*
and the *Wrath which is cruel;* and that they use not *Instruments of
Cruelty in their Habitations.*" As a reminder of their duty, he pic-
tured Cheever as speaking to them from on high:

[56] Sewall, "Diary," I, 225, 369.
[57] Cotton Mather, *Magnalia*, I, 445.

> TUTORS, Be *Strict;* But yet be *Gentle* too:
> Don't by fierce *Cruelties* fair *Hopes* undo.
> Dream not, that they who are to Learning slow,
> Will mend by Arguments in *Ferio.*
> Who keeps the *Golden Fleece,* Oh, let him not
> A *Dragon* be, tho' he *Three Tongues* have got.
> Why can you not to Learning find the way,
> But thro' the Province of *Severia?*
> Twas *Moderatus,* who taught *Origen;*
> A *Youth* which prov'd one of the Best of men.
> The Lads with *Honour* first, and *Reason* Rule;
> *Blowes* are but for the *Refractory Fool.*[58]

In his own family Cotton Mather endeavored to follow the principles which he so evidently approved. Concerning his disciplinary methods he wrote in his diary:

> The *first Chastisement,* which I inflict for an ordinary Fault, is, to lett the Child see and hear me in an Astonishment, and hardly able to beleeve that the Child could do so *base* a Thing, but beleeving that they will never do it again.
>
> I would never come, to give a child a *Blow;* except in Case of *Obstinacy:* or some gross Enormity.
>
> To be chased for a while out of *my Presence,* I would make to be look'd upon, as the sorest Punishment in the Family. . . .
>
> The *slavish* way of *Education,* carried on with raving and kicking and scourging (in *Schools* as well as *Families,*) tis abominable; and a dreadful Judgment of God upon the World.[59]

Thomas Cobbett had the same opinion of the "slavish way of education." He advised parents to make commands to their children in "pathetical" terms, "namely in the most moving expressions, which may help on affectionate attendance and observance thereof."[60] These statements provide the gloss for Mather's epigram on the value of whipping. Though it was better to be whipped than damned, it was still better to be presuaded than whipped. In reading the Puritan praises of the rod, it is necessary to remember that

[58] Cotton Mather, *Corderius Americanus,* pp. 20–21, 32.
[59] Cotton Mather, "Diary," I, 535–536.
[60] Cobbett, *Frutifull Discourse,* p. 118.

they regarded it as a last resort. They saved their highest approval
for a much more intelligent method of discipline, a method which
depended for its efficacy upon the development of a special attitude
in the child and upon a thorough understanding by the parent of
each child's peculiar personality.

Every Puritan child was taught to reverence his parents. William
Ames pointed out that "Parents in regard to their Children, doe
beare a singular image of God, as hee is the Creatour, Sustainer,
and Governour";[61] and Thomas Cobbett advised children to "Present your Parents so to your minds, as bearing the Image of Gods
Father-hood, and that also will help on your filiall awe and Reverence to them." According to Cobbett, filial reverence consisted of a
holy respect and fear both of a parent's person and of his words; a
reverent child felt ashamed of his faults before his parents; he
feared to lose their favor, feared to cross their just interests, feared
to grieve them or fall short of their expectations. Moreover, he displayed these fears in his outward actions. When he spoke to his
parents, he stood up because "It stands not with Parents Honour,
for children to sit and speak, but rather they should stand up when
they speak to Parents." If he saw his parents approaching him, he
went to meet them and bowed to them; he spoke reverently to them
and of them, and to express his sense of shame for his faults, he
blushed and confessed his unworthiness when they corrected him.[62]
But reverence was more than fear and awe: it was also a matter of
love. When a child had the proper reverence for his parents, he
mixed his fear with affection. His parents naturally loved him, the
Puritans said, and it was his duty to love them in return (though
each must reserve his highest love for God). If, however, he were to
show them the same kind of affection that they showed him, he
would be considered too familiar and assuming. Thomas Cobbett
warned parents not to meet their children on equal grounds or to
display too great visible affection. Wise parents would keep a "due
distance" between their children and themselves, because they

[61] William Ames, *Conscience with the Power and Cases thereof* (London,
1643), Book V, p. 159.
[62] Cobbett, *Fruitfull Discourse*, pp. 90–99.

knew that "fondness and familiarity breeds and causeth contempt and irreverence in children."[63] When Jane, the gifted daughter of Benjamin Colman, showed herself a little too effusive in letters to her father, she recognized the fact and asked his pardon. He gave it along with some advice for the prevention of such conduct:

You ask me to forgive the Flow of your Affections, which run with so swift a Current of filial Duty as may carry you beyond yourself sometimes, and make you wanting in that Respect which you aim at expressing. It is true, my Dear, that a young fond and musical Genius is easily carry'd away thus; and never more than when it runs into the Praises of what it loves; and I would have you therefore careful against this Error, even when you say your Thoughts of Reverence and Esteem to your Father, or to a Spouse, if ever you should live to have one. It is easy to be lavish and run into foolish Flatteries. I think you have done well to correct yourself for some of your Excursions of this kind toward me.[64]

Though the mark of the eighteenth century is clearly upon this letter, especially in the application of its doctrines to spouse as well as father, it sufficiently illustrates the point which Cobbett had made in 1656.

If a child acted toward his parents with the proper combination of fear and love, discipline would be a simple matter, for "we easyly obey them whom we reverence";[65] but not all children would readily fall into a reverential attitude, and proper discipline of those who did not required careful attention to each child's abilities and temperament. Though filial reverence kept the child at a respectful distance, his parents had to have a close understanding of his particular personality in order to know how to treat him. As Anne Bradstreet put it: "Diverse children have their different natures; some are like flesh which nothing but salt will keep from putrefaction; some again like tender fruits that are best preserved with sugar: those parents are wise that can fit their nurture according to

---

[63] Cobbett, *Fruitfull Discourse*, p. 96.
[64] Ebenezer Turell, *Memoirs of the Life and Death of the Pious and Ingenious Mrs. Jane Turell* (London, 1741), p. 16.
[65] Boston Sermons, Sept. 30, 1672.

their Nature."[66] In accordance with this principle Samuel Willard advised parents to "Know their natural inclinations, dispositions [and] use severity as the last means," while Cotton Mather told schoolmasters that they should "prudently study the *Tempers* of the Children, they have to deal withal."[67] Parents and schoolmasters who did so could warn each child against the sins to which he seemed most susceptible. Before a bad habit could take hold, they would be able to suppress it, and thus prevent custom from supporting sin:

When Parents by wise observations do perceive the bent, and bias of their Children, now let them carry it towards them accordingly. If they be strongly bent to some vice more than others, as Lying . . . admonish them betimes in the evill of it, represent to them what God speaketh, in especiall wise against it, what sad examples and sequels, in Scripture and otherwise, both in poynt of sin, and in point of judgements, are found, thereof: after which course taken, then watch them the more narrowly, and spare them not for it, if they fall into lying again. . . .

But on the other hand, "if Children, either by common, or saving influences of the Spirit, are more ingenuous spirits, and of better and more hopefull dispositions, Oh let parents, as they discern the same, incourage the same, all the prudent and pious wayes that may be. . . ."[68]

Here is no disposition to allow the unimpeded development of personality, but at least children were not subjected to a preconceived discipline without reference to their individual needs and capacities. A parent in order to educate his children properly had to know them well, to understand their particular characters, and to treat them accordingly. Granted its purposes and assumptions, Puritan education was intelligently planned, and the relationship between parent and child which it envisaged was not one of harshness and severity but of tenderness and sympathy.

[66] Anne Bradstreet, *Works*, p. 50.
[67] Boston Sermons, Sept. 21, 1679; and Cotton Mather, *Corderius Americanus*, p. 20.
[68] Cobbett, *Fruitfull Discourse*, pp. 219–221.

V

Masters
and Servants

$\mathcal{M}$OST of the inhabitants of seventeenth-century New England either were or had been "servants." Today the word "servant" usually means a domestic: the cook, the butler, the chambermaid. In the seventeenth century it meant anyone who worked for another in whatever capacity, in industry, commerce, or agriculture, as well as in what we now call domestic economy. For example, Henry Dispaw and his son were known in Lynn, Massachusetts, as the servants of John Gifford, because they ran an iron foundry for him there. They were nevertheless among the richest people in town, for their wages amounted to £35 per year apiece, besides their lodgings.[1] On the other hand, Negro and Indian slaves were also known as servants, and so were apprentices. Servants, then, might differ considerably in their economic and social status.

They differed also in serving either voluntarily or involuntarily. Most servants in New England were voluntary: they had agreed of their own free will to serve someone else, usually for a sum of money. It required capital to set up in business or trade for oneself, and the easiest way of acquiring capital, apart from stealing, was to work for wages as a "hired servant." Another reason, which led perhaps a majority of the population into servitude in their youth, was the need of education: a child might agree, with the consent and guidance of his parents, to work as an "apprentice" for seven years or more in order to learn some trade.[2] Still another reason for

[1] *Essex Court Records*, VI, 80–82.
[2] See ch. III above.

109

becoming a servant was to get across the ocean. A man who wished
to come to New England but who had no money to pay for passage
might agree to serve a master for seven years in return for the cost
of the voyage. He thereby became an "indentured" or "covenant"
servant. Voluntary servants might be hired, apprenticed, or
indentured.

Involuntary servants worked for a master as punishment for
wrongdoing. The Puritans punished several kinds of delinquency
in this way. The first kind was making war—on the wrong side.
Prisoners taken in a just war, it was held, had forfeited their own
lives by their attempt to take the lives of others; their punishment
must be either death or slavery. On this ground the Puritans en-
slaved the Indians whom they captured in the Pequot War and in
King Philip's War. Many of these Indians they sold in the West
Indies and in return brought back Negroes (captured, presumably,
in equally just wars), for Negroes were more docile than Pequots
or Mohawks or Narrangansetts.[3] Irishmen and Scotsmen taken by
Cromwell's armies were likewise shipped to New England by en-
terprising dealers, there to expiate the resistance of their nations at
Dublin and Dunbar.[4] The Irish and Scots, however, must have
been thought less culpable than the Indians or the Negroes, for they
seem to have served not for life but only for a few years. A bill of
sale, dated May 10, 1654, states that George Dell, master of the
ship *Goodfellow,* sold to Samuel Symonds for the sum of twenty-
six pounds "two of the Irish youthes I brought over by order of the
State of England." They were to serve for nine years. Another
paper indicates that Dell, doubtless out of magnanimity to Symonds, later extended the time to eleven years.[5]

The Puritans did not, however, uphold the slavery of all captives.
Kidnapers who supplied the Barbados and other colonies with

[3] For Puritan views on slavery see Willard, *Compleat Body of Divinity,* p.
614; George H. Moore, *Notes on the History of Slavery in Massachusetts*
(New York, 1866), pp. 1–10, 32, 251–256. Cf. John Locke, *Two Treatises of
Government,* ed. Peter Laslett (Cambridge, 1964), pp. 301–303.

[4] Peter Ross, *The Scot in America* (New York, 1896) pp. 48–49.

[5] *Essex Court Records,* II, 295.

servants were less successful in New England. The Body of Liberties provided that "there shall never be any bond-slavery, villenage or captivitie amongst us; unlesse it be lawfull captives, taken in just warrs, and such strangers[6] as willingly sell themselves or are solde to us."[7] In accordance with this provision Robert Collins, who had been kidnaped and brought to New England in 1672, was upheld by the Suffolk County Court when he refused to serve the man who had brought him.[8] Slaves were comparatively few in New England homes in the seventeenth century, though the number increased rapidly in the eighteenth.[9]

Misdeeds less vicious than that of choosing the wrong side in a war were also occasionally punished by servitude. When a man stole from, or otherwise damaged, another and could not make restitution in cash, he might be sold for a number of years to pay the bill.[10] The courts frequently made him restore double or triple the value of the damage as punishment (the law called for triple restitution). For example: when Owen Jones was convicted "of stealing a rugg and a coate from Phillip Keane valued at twenty six Shillings," the court ordered that he make threefold restitution and "in case hee make not Satisfaction accordingly that hee bee Sold";[11] Benjamin Barker, who obtained three pounds from Mrs. Lydia Scottow under false pretences, was sentenced to be sold for a period

[6] This word was omitted in the 1660 and 1672 editions of the Massachusetts codebook. George H. Moore claims that the omission was made deliberately in order that the children of slaves might be retained in the same status as their parents. See *Notes on the History of Slavery*, pp. 10–30.

[7] *Massachusetts Laws of 1648*, p. 4.

[8] *Suffolk Court Records*, pp. 18–20, 43–44. See also the case in which Captain Smith and Mr. Keser were punished for stealing Negroes in Africa and the Negroes ordered to be returned (John Winthrop, *The History of New England*, II, 243–245, and Appendix M).

[9] Governor Bradstreet's letter to the Lords of Trade, May 18, 1680 (Massachusetts Historical Society *Collections*, third series, VIII, 337) reported few slaves in Massachusetts, but by 1754 they numbered 4,489 (J. B. Felt, "Statistics of Population in Massachusetts," American Statistical Association *Collections*, I, 208).

[10] E.g., *Suffolk Court Records*, pp. 631, 886, 1014, 1015, 1066.

[11] *Suffolk Court Records*, p. 631.

of not more than four years in order to pay her six pounds as double restitution;[12] and when Henry Stevens, a servant of Mr. John Humfrey, set fire to his master's barn, he was "ordered to bee servant to Mr. Humfrey for 21 years from this day, toward recompencing the losse."[13] Another kind of damage which could be restored by servitude was debt. According to New England laws, when a man could not pay his debts, the creditor could exact his due (but not double or triple his due) in service. The Essex County Court Records contain copies of several executions delivering debtors to their creditors as servants.[14]

Obviously these various types of servants worked for their masters on different terms. A hired servant, for example, enjoyed many more advantages than a slave.[15] Yet religion, which guided all human relations in seventeenth-century New England, made no distinction between servants. When the Puritan God gave his approbation to servitude, he gave "necessary Rules, prescribing and limiting the Duties belonging to this Relation,"[16] and in those rules he did not assign different duties to different servants. To all alike he commanded three things: obedience, faithfulness, and reverence, so that in theory all servants had the same duties and bore the same relationship to their masters.

The Puritan ministers never tired of inculcating obedience. It made no difference, they said, whether the master was kind or unkind, harsh or lenient; his servants must obey every command, "because the primary ground of this duty is not the merit of Masters, but the ordinance of God."[17] Benjamin Wadsworth advised servants that "when your Master or Mistress bids you do this or

---

[12] Ibid., p. 886.

[13] *Massachusetts Records*, I, 311.

[14] *Eessex Court Records*, VI, 393, 394, 395; VII, 324–325; VIII, 441.

[15] Doubtless many hired servants worked for their master by day but returned to a home of their own at night. These need not concern us, for they were not members of their master's family, nor were they under his "family government."

[16] Willard, *Compleat Body of Divinity*, p. 614.

[17] William Ames, *Conscience*, p. 160.

that, *Christ* bids you do it, because he bids you obey them: therefore do what's bidden, out of obedience to Christ, as to him and for
him."[18] Faithfulness was equally important. Since a servant was
employed in his master's interests, not his own, he must consider
his master's welfare in every action. Whether he was carrying out a
specific command or following his own discretion, he must ask himself, *"Which way may my Master become the better for me?"*[19] The
remaining duty, reverence, naturally induced obedience and faithfulness. The reverence of a servant was supposed to surpass that of
wives and children in containing a greater element of fear. All in-
feriors were expected to fear their superiors, but as Samuel Willard
put it, "this Fear is diversifyed according to the Nature of the Relation which they stand in: the Apostle therefore here subjoyns
trembling, to express the kind of Fear belonging to Men in this
Order, implying a sense of their Subjection, and the Power their
Masters have over them."[20] Servants who feared their masters with
a holy fear and trembling would never dare disobey them or betray
their interests.

The Puritans did not rely on reverence alone, however, to secure
the obedience and faithfulness of servants. Since corrupt human
nature inevitably tended against the fulfillment of these duties, the
courts were kept busy asserting and enforcing them, for the courts
never failed to support the dictates of religion. The first code of
laws in Massachusetts, printed in 1648, made these regulations:

It is ordered by this Court and the Authoritie therof, that no
servant, either man or maid shall either give, sell or *truck* any com-
moditie whatsoever without licence from their Masters, during the
time of their service under pain of Fine, or corporal punishment at
the discretion of the Court as the offence shall deserve.

2 And that all workmen shall work the whole day allowing convenient time for food and rest.

3 It is also ordered that when any servants shall run from their

[18] Wadsworth, *Well-Ordered Family*, p. 115.
[19] Cotton Mather, *A Good Master well Served* (Boston, 1696), p. 46.
[20] Willard, *Compleat Body of Divinity*, p. 616.

masters, or any other Inhabitants shall privily goe away with suspicion of ill intentions, it shall be lawfull for the next Magistrate, or
the Constable and two of the chief Inhabitants where no Magistrate is to presse men and boats or pinnaces at the publick charge
to pursue such persons by Sea or Land and bring them back by
force of Arms.[21]

Other laws forbade tavern keepers to entertain servants and
shipmasters to take them on board.[22] The courts went beyond the
laws. They punished not only the servants who neglected their
duties but also the persons who encouraged servants to do so;[23] and
they demanded that masters be given respect as well as obedience.
James Morgan was admonished "for his abusive words and carriages to his master,"[24] while Elizabeth Iago of Newbury was presented by the grand jury simply "for wishing that the devil had
Mary Lad and all the company, in which company was her master."[25] Legislative and judicial action thus gave official support to
the authority which masters exercised over their servants. It was
not necessary, however, for a master to seek assistance from the
government whenever his servants proved unruly, for he himself
had the right to chastise any servant who refused to obey his commands both faithfully and reverently.

The life of a servant, therefore, whether he served voluntarily or
involuntarily, was anything but pleasant. He must do nothing without his master's consent or command. He must work the whole day
at whatever task his master assigned him, and even at night he
could not count his time his own. He must be at beck and call during every hour of the twenty-four. If he did his duty, he could have
no time for a private life, except what his master out of pure magnanimity might allow him—and masters who were trying to build
a home and earn a living in the wilderness were not likely to be
magnanimous. If the servant were undutiful and tried to steal time
for private affairs, he faced punishment, either by his master or by

---

[21] *Massachusetts Laws of 1648*, p. 38.
[22] *Massachusetts Laws of 1672*, pp. 27, 281.
[23] E.g., *Essex Court Records*, VIII, 12; IV, 151, 170.
[24] *Suffolk Court Records*, p. 631.
[25] *Essex Court Records*, VI, 138.

the state. His condition would have been all but insupportable if it had not been mitigated by a number of factors: by the limitations which religion and law placed upon the master's authority, by the compensation which a servant could demand for his services, by the practical power which a servant might wield (as opposed to his theoretical helplessness) to gain some time for himself, and lastly by the fact that most servants could regard their condition as temporary.

God, according to the Puritans, gave masters authority in order that they might use it "in furthering their Servants in a blameless behaviour; and in restraining them from Sin."[26] Like all authority, a master's was limited and defined by the laws of God. He could not rightfully command of his servants any evil action. If he did, "they must humbly refuse; for both their Masters and they are God's Servants, and they must not disobey Him to please Men."[27] Furthermore, the courts would punish a wicked master just as they punished an undutiful servant. For example, if a master took advantage of his position to force unwanted attentions on a maidservant, he received severe punishment. John Harris and his son Joseph were both whipped twenty stripes and imprisoned when John's maid complained to the Middlesex County Court that they had made forcible attempts against her chastity.[28] Because of a master's power to intimidate a servant, the courts seem generally to have favored the servant in cases of this kind. The Middlesex County Court did so when Sarah Lepingwell complained that Thomas Hawes, her master's brother, had violated her, and that she had forborne to call for help because she "was posesed with fear of my master least my master shold think I did it only to bring a scandall on his brother and thinking thay wold all beare witnes agaynst me." Sarah was right in fearing that the rest of the family would bear witness against her; yet, in spite of their testimony, Hawes was found guilty.[29]

[26] Wadsworth, *Well-Ordered Family*, p. 106.
[27] Willard, *Compleat Body of Divinity*, p. 616.
[28] Middlesex Files, folder 94, group 3.
[29] Middlesex Files, folder 47, group 3.

Even when a master's commands were righteous, he could not enforce them by cruel methods. With servants as with children the Puritans discountenanced harshness where softer means would avail. As Willard put it, "Extreme Rigour here is extream wrong . . . we are not to make Asses of our Servants, whilst they may be treated as Men."[30] Cotton Mather pointed out that the punishment of a disobedient servant should be so "moderated with Humanity, that he may not be thereby *Killed,* or *Maimed: Eye for Eye, Tooth for Tooth, and Life for Life,* will be demanded, by the Righteous God, the Judge of the Creepled Servant."[31] And before God demanded justice, the courts might do so. When Philip Fowler was presented at the Essex County Court for abusing his servant, the court affirmed that they "justified any person in giving meet correction to his servant, which the boy deserved, yet they did not approve of the manner of punishment given in hanging him up by the heels as butchers do beasts for the slaughter, and cautioned said Fowler against such kind of punishment."[32] If a master's punishments maimed or disfigured his servants, the law required that they be set free—and many servants were set free when they proved that their masters had beaten them excessively. For example, in December 1640 the General Court of Massachusetts declared that "Samuel Hefford haveing bene much misused by his master, Jonathan Wade, hee is freed from the said Mr. Wade, and is put to John Johnson for three yeares, and to have £6 wages per annum."[33] Sometimes masters were themselves punished for abusing their servants. Edward Messenger was sentenced to be severely whipped "for his unmercifullnes towards his Servant and lying to extenuet his fault,"[34] and Nathaniel Wells was fined simply for "abusive speeches to his servants." The words he used were comparatively mild: "old rogue, old witch, and old wizard."[35]

[30] Willard, *Compleat Body of Divinity*, p. 615.
[31] Cotton Mather, *A Good Master well Served*, p. 16.
[32] *Essex Court Records*, VIII, 302–303.
[33] *Massachusetts Records*, I, 311.
[34] "Records of the Particular Court of Connecticut," in Connecticut Historical Society *Collections*, XXII, 119.
[35] *Essex Court Records*, V, 232.

All servants shared this right to decent treatment, just as all shared the duties of obedience, faithfulness, and reverence. They differed, however, in the rewards received for their services. A master was required to give a certain basic minimum to all, but beyond that, as already observed, he gave different kinds of compensation to different kinds of servants. The minimum was care for the servant's bodily existence and spiritual welfare. It was a master's duty to provide food, clothing, and shelter (though hired servants usually paid for these out of their wages), and the courts saw to it that he did. For example, in May 1685 Benjamin Mills was ordered to appear at the Middlesex Court to answer for the fact that his Indian boy was not sufficiently clothed.[36] Bodily necessities included, besides food, clothing, and shelter, care in sickness. When Hugh March's master failed to take proper care of him during an illness, Hugh's father took him home and later recovered twenty pounds damages from the master.[37] Much more important than bodily health, however, was spiritual health. A master was expected to take as much care of his servants' souls as he did of his children's. "Do *This* for your Servants," Cotton Mather urged,

Leave them not Unacquainted with, and Uncatechised in, the *PRINCIPLES OF RELIGION*. Let your *Servants* be able to say of you, as in Math. 22. 16. *Master, Thou Teachest the way of God, in Truth;* and let them not be Ignorant of any Saving Truth. Again Do *This* for your Servants; ENQUIRE critically into their Spiritual Estate before God. Be prudently Inquisitive into their *Experiences,* into their *Temptations,* into their *Behaviours.* Further, Do *This* for your Servants; REPROVE every Miscarriage that may be Discerned in them. Show them all the *Paths of the Destroyer,* whereto they may be Inclining, and Lovingly, Solemnly, Scripturally Chide them out of those *Paths.*[38]

Every householder, being "a sort of Priest in his Family," was bound to seek the salvation of the souls under his charge, the souls of servants as well as of children. According to Willard, "All the

---

[36] Middlesex Files, folder 114, group 1.
[37] *Essex Court Records,* V, 417–419.
[38] Cotton Mather, *A Good Master well Served,* pp. 17–18.

Members in a Family are therein equal, in that they have Souls equally capable of being saved or lost: And the Soul of a Slave is, in its nature, of as much worth, as the Soul of his Master."[39] The Puritan churches expressed their concurrence with Willard on this point, showing no discrimination between master and servant in admissions to the church. Samuel Sewall recorded on December 16, 1711, "Four persons were taken into the church. Mrs. Frances Bromfield and Marshal's Negro woman, two of them. Their Relations very acceptable."[40] And Cotton Mather was proud to write in his diary on April 21, 1700:

> This day, my *Servant*, was offered unto the Communion of my Church. But in the Account that she gave to the Church of her Conversion, she Declared her living in my Family to have been the Means of it, and that she should forever bless God for bringing her under my Roof.
>
> Others of my Servants formerly (and almost all that ever lived with me,) have joined unto my church, while they have lived with mee; and blessed God for their Living in my poor sinful Family.[41]

The civil government protected the spiritual welfare of servants by commanding masters to catechise them. It also forbade work on the Sabbath, required all persons to attend church, and sometimes even held masters responsible for the attendance of their servants. Walter Fearffield was admonished in 1673 "for detaining or in not requiring his servant John Besoon to attend the public worship of God on the Lord's day."[42]

The compensation which a servant received beyond the care of his soul and body depended upon what type of servant he was. A slave, of course, received nothing more. Neither did a servant who served for debt or for a crime. An indentured servant, however, might expect a set of tools and a suit of clothing at the end of his term. Such was the meaning of the General Court of Massachusetts

---

[39] Willard, *Compleat Body of Divinity*, p. 616.
[40] Samuel Sewall, "Diary," II, 329.
[41] Cotton Mather, "Diary," I, 346–347.
[42] *Essex Court Records*, V, 221.

when it provided that "all servants that have served diligently and faithfully to the benefit of their Masters seven years shall not be sent away emptie."[43] Those who got most for their efforts were hired servants and apprentices. The hired servant not only received additional compensation in the form of wages, but he enjoyed a higher rate of compensation than other servants. Whereas an indentured servant worked for seven years to repay a service worth only six pounds (the usual fare for passage to America),[44] a hired servant could earn that much in a year, besides his bed and board. Samuel Sewall noted the wages of a woman domestic servant as two shillings a week, besides board and room, which would make five pounds and four shillings in a single year, while a bill of charges for day labor, preserved in the files of the Middlesex County Court, shows that some laborers received two shillings a day.[45] Other evidence indicates that when a servant continued to live with his master after his period of indenture had elapsed, he could earn in two days of the week the charges for his board and room.[46] The rest of the week's work was clear gain over his former condition. The two Irishmen who had been sold to Samuel Symonds easily perceived the difference between this condition of things and their own. After they had served seven years, they rebelled. Another servant narrated in court that one night the pair

came into the parlor to prayer with the rest of the family, and Philip asked if Goodman Bragg's son was coming to plow tomorrow. Her mistress said she thought so, that he said he would consider it. Philip then asked who would plow with him and her mistress said, "One of you." Philip said, "We will worke with you, or for you, noe longer." Then said my master, is it soe? What will you play? Then both of them stood in it and expressed that it was soe,

[43] *Massachusetts Laws of 1648*, p. 39.

[44] George L. Beer, *The Origins of the British Colonial System* (New York, 1908), p. 49.

[45] Samuel Sewall, "Letter-Book," Massachusetts Historical Society *Collections*, sixth series, I, 270; Middlesex Files, folder 13, group 3.

[46] *Essex Court Records*, II, 308; Middlesex Files, folder 59, group 4 (case of Thomas Hinshaw).

and that they had been with you (speaking to my master) longe enough. we have served you seaven yeares, we thinke that is longe enough; Then said my master But we must not be our owne Judges; and said my master you must worke for me still, unles you run away. Then said william, we scorne to run away. Then said Philip, we will goe away, and leave you before your faces. Alsoe they did both speak to this purpose; If you will free us, we will plant your corne, and mende your fences, and if you will pay us as other men, but we will not worke with you upon the same termes, or conditions as before.[47]

Apprentices received less immediate gain from their labors than did the hired servants, but they could count on their training to enhance the value of their labor in the future. They were usually boys under twenty-one and girls under eighteen who had been placed out by their parents according to the custom discussed already.[48] The work they performed was less valuable than that of an adult but sufficient to repay their masters for maintaining and educating them.

The contract by which a child became an apprentice followed a form established in the Middle Ages. The Boston Almanack for 1692 printed a model:

The form of an Indenture for an Apprentice.

This Indenture witnesseth, that *Henry Nap,* Son of *Joseph Nap,* of *Boston,* in the County of *Suffolk,* Ship Carpenter, hath put himself, and by these presents doth voluntarily put himself Apprentice to *William Stone* of *Charlstown, Butcher;* to learn his Art, after the manner of an Apprentice to serve him from the day of the date hereof, for and during the term of seven years, thence next following: During all which term, the said Apprentice his said Master faithfully shall serve, his secrets keep, his lawful commandments every where obey, He shall do no damage to his said Master, nor seen to be done of others, without letting or giving notice thereof to his said Master: He shall not waste his said Masters Goods, nor lend them unlawfully to any; he shall not commit Fornication, nor

---

[47] *Essex Court Records,* II, 296–297.
[48] See chapter III above.

contract Matrimony within the said term; at Cards, Dice, or any unlawful Game he shall not play, whereby his Master may have damage with his own Goods or others: He shall not absent himself day or night from his Masters service without his leave, nor haunt Ale house, nor Tavern, but in all things behave himself as a faithful Apprentice ought to do; during all the said term, And the said *Master* shall use the utmost of his endeavour, to teach or cause to be taught or instructed, his said Aprentice in the Trade or *Mystery* that he now followeth; and to find and provide for him sufficient meat, drink, apparel, lodging and washing befitting an Apprentice, during all the said term. And for the true performance of all and every the said Covenants and Agreements either of the said parties binds himself unto the other by these presents. In witness whereof, they have interchangeably set their hands the 10th day of *April,* &c.[49]

The terms of this contract are almost exactly those of the earliest known contracts of the thirteenth and fourteenth centuries.[50] The child received food, clothing, lodging, and an education in the art or "mystery" of his master's trade. In addition the laws of New England entitled him to instruction in reading and religion.[51] Actual contracts, varying in details from the model just given, frequently provided that the servant should receive two suits of clothing, a sum of money, and sometimes a set of tools at the end of his term. Occasionally he was also promised instruction in writing, to accompany the instruction in reading that the laws demanded for him. Thomas Drabrucke contracted for most of these rewards when he became the apprentice of John Fleming, a maltster, on June 8, 1654:

And the sayd John Fleming and hes wife for the sayd Thomas ther servant shall provid dureinge the sayd forme of yeaight yeares sufisient meate drinke Lodgeinge washing hoase shus Linning wolling and to teach hem or case hem to be taht to writt and rede and to bee instructed in the grounds of religion and all things nesessary

[49] H. B. (Benjamin Harrison), *Boston Almanack for the year of our Lord God 1692* (Boston, 1692), in pages at the end.

[50] See Robert F. Seybolt, *Apprenticeship and Apprenticeship Education in Colonial New England and New York* (New York, 1917), pp 12–13.

[51] See chapter IV above.

for such an a printise as well in sicknes as in helth: and shall att the
end terme of yeaight yeares give him yeaight pound of Currant
marchantabell pay: and to give hem two suits of aparrell of
Lininge wollinge hoase shues and hatts one for working days and
the other fitt for saboth days.[52]

The fact that an apprentice had to be taught a particular trade
prescribed the kind of work in which he would ordinarily be employed. If he was to learn, say, the art of a maltster, he could not be
occupied regularly in tending sheep or ploughing a field. Occasionally contracts specifically provided against such an eventuality. For
example, when Luke Perkins apprenticed himself to Samuel Carter,
a shoemaker, he stipulated "that the sayd samuell cartar the mais-
ter or his Assignes shall not exceed above six weeks in a year to
employ the sayd Luke Perkins from his Calling of a shoemaker
unto any other employments."[53] Although Samuel Buckman's contract with John Atkinson, a feltmaker, contained no such clause,
Buckman recovered damages when it was sworn in court that Atkinson "several times let out Samuel Buckman to husbandry work
and employed him a great deal in that work himself."[54] Governor
Bellingham himself took the case of John Slater in hand and directed the following order to the constable of Concord:

Whereas I am informed that One John Slater Sonne [of] John
Slater of Surrey Feltmaker was brought over as an apprentice to be
taught a certain Trade, and alsoe that the said John the younger is
sold often from one too another without respect to his trade
whereby the said youth is much wronged These are therefore to
require you to find out the said John Slater beinge dwelling in your
Towne as is reported and bringe him to the next Court at Cambridge that his case may be examined and right may be done ac-
cordinge to Lawe and hereof fayle not at your perill Dat 23th 1
month 1650/51.[55]

---

[52] Middlesex Files, folder 18, group 5. Cf. Seybolt, *Apprenticeship and Apprenticeship Education*, pp. 36–51.
[53] Middlesex Files, folder 26, group 2.
[54] *Essex Court Records*, VIII, 249–250.
[55] Middlesex Files, folder 19, group 4.

A servant could console himself with the fact that his master could not beat him unmercifully. If a slave, he could be thankful he had been allowed to live; if an indentured servant, that he had been brought to New England whither he had wished to come. If a hired servant, he could think of his wages, and if an apprentice, of the education he was receiving. Yet none of these consolations would alter the plain fact that he had no right to a private life. If he did his duty as he ought, his time, day and night, was all his master's. Unless he were a good Puritan, however, he would not be likely to take his duties seriously except for fear of punishment. On this very ground the ministers consistently urged the heads of families to teach their servants religion and not to take profane ones into their families if they could avoid it.[56] Even so, it was apparently difficult to get pious ones, for the evidence indicates that most New England servants were not good Puritans. Though they had as much right to join the church as their masters did, the records show that not many actually did join. Ezekiel Rogers complained in 1658 that it was "hard to get a *servant* that is glad of *catechising,* or *family-duties:* I had a rare blessing of servants in Yorkshire; and those that I brought over were a blessing: but the *young brood* doth much afflict me."[57] Without religious scruples to make them obedient, faithful, and reverent, servants could exercise considerable power in their own behalf. There was a large borderland between absolute dutifulness and punishable wrongdoing where, by the threat of minor annoyances, an unscrupulous servant could win concessions from his master. Thomas Hooker described what must have been a common practice: "My Master rebuked me sharply saies the Servant, . . . but I think I fitted them, they would have their way and wil, and would have it done after their manner, And I did it with a witness, so il-favoredly, that I know it vexed al the veyns of their hearts, thats the way to weary them. . . ."[58]

Servants sometimes displayed great ingenuity in devising ways

---

[56] Cotton Mather, *A Good Master well Served*, p. 9.
[57] Cotton Mather, *Magnalia Christi Americana*, I, 413.
[58] Thomas Hooker, *The Application of Redemption*, p. 429.

to annoy their masters. Mehitable Brabrook, for example, took revenge for a scolding, as she later confessed to a fellow servant, by putting "a great toad" into a kettle of milk.[59] Mehitable later committed more serious damage by setting the house on fire when shaking the ashes out of her pipe. A master who wished to save his house from fire and his goods from theft had to make some effort to win the good will of his servants, for he frequently had to leave them alone in the house, and unless they loved and respected him, no amount of care would secure the cupboard or the cellar against them. The court records show that many thefts were committed by servants, and that a major part of them occurred on Sundays when the rest of the family was dutifully attending church. Sometimes a child stole from his master in behalf of his parents. John Pulcipher confessed in May 1679

that he lived with Mr. Francis Wainwright the last winter and his father and mother told him that they wanted wheat which he might help them to, whereupon he carried to them about a half bushel of wheat which he took from Mr. Wainwright's chamber and delivered it to his father at his own house. His mother made a cake and gave him. Later he took a bushel of wheat and they asking him for pork, he took two large pieces five or six times, from his master's warehouse, and cut out a small hog, half a bushel of salt, two bundles of candles, and about 5 li. sugar at two times in a handkerchief, also three or four times he carried three or four hogsleaves at a time, all of which his father and mother received.[60]

One bold servant, Nathaniel King, stole twelve pounds from his master's cupboard, used three pounds toward buying his freedom, "affirming it was mony sent him by his mother from England," gave three pounds to another servant for the same purpose, four pounds to an accomplice, and spent the rest at various ordinaries treating his friends to wine and cakes.[61]

A factor adding to the servant's boldness in New England was

---

[59] *Essex Court Records*, IV, 56–57.
[60] Ibid., VII, 264.
[61] Middlesex Files, folder 56, group 6.

the scarcity of labor. Since hands were few, a master needed all the work he could get out of his servants; yet if they bore him a grudge and did every task "ill-favoredly," in the manner that Hooker described, he would be little the better for them. Strictness might even lead them to run away at a crucial time, perhaps at harvest, and even though he recovered them and had their term of service extended by the court, he would not be able to repair his immediate loss. One servant was provoked to run away, as he himself implied in a confession to the court, simply because he was "dealt with" by his mistress for attempting to seduce her ten-year-old daughter.[62] The fact that his master sought his return after such an incident is proof in itself of the demand for labor. A master would hesitate to ask assistance from the state against an unruly servant, because the punishment inflicted by the courts might keep the servant from his work for a considerable time, especially if it involved imprisonment. One servant who was imprisoned for attempting an escape to Jamaica took advantage of the demand for labor and continued to defy his master even from prison, for the master complained that "by the Countenance and Supply of some Contentious persons hee hath Sett up and practices his Trade [in prison] refuseing to returne again To your petitioners Imployment."[63]

The power of labor did not often take such graphic expression, but it did give servants more practical independence than they should have enjoyed theoretically. The amount of insubordination which a master would put up with before complaining to the authorities is indicated by the petitions which were filed when a servant's misdemeanors finally became insufferable. Here is a list of "Some miscarreages of John Creete," filed by his master in the Middlesex County Court:

first verie often Lying out on night times without Leave and against my Express charge to the Contrary in indian harvest time.
2. taking my horse and riding out both by night and day without my knowledge

---

[62] Ibid., folder 11, group 3 (case of John Glazier).
[63] *Suffolk Court Records*, p. 801.

3. often going abroad to Charlst and Boston without my knowledge as on the 8th month 24 day to Charlstown with 1 bushel of
indian and stayed out two days. dec 11th against my Express
mind to Boston as he sayd to fetch A Letter which was one
whole day.

27 dec. he went out in A Cold night on no occasion of mine after
which he kept his bed and Lay by 4 days on fitts he cald Ague fitts.
the like he did on 2 and 3d of the 11th month.

and allso the 10th and 11th of the same

24 and 25 he was out two whole nights and the Last of them came
about break of day and broke into my kitchin at the window.

allso on the 26 of the 8 month he went to Charlestown and sett A
warrant for Pater Tufts without my knowledge.

28 11 he went away about daylight without my knowledge and
stayed till night.

27 1st month against Express order in planting time he went away
and Came not home till after bedtime.

moreover on the 9th of the 11th month when he went to Mill he
stole Sold and Conveyed away two pounds and A half of Tobacco.
sold for 12d to Samuel Carter.

more one pound of Tobacco sold Samuel Peirce.[64]

Another servant, "Jeeameel Bowers," showed a similar spirit of independence; his misdemeanors included the following:

Jn hay time last when his Master set him to makinge of hay he
tooke an other mans hors and Rod him about the woods. . . . Jn
huskinge time he went out all night without any leave of his Master
and Cam not whome till the next day and when his Master re-
proved him he went out the next night in contempt and Cam not
whom till the next day after. The Select men haveinge a meetinge
his Master had him before them to see if he could convent him and
all hee had to say was that he did not know the law and he hoped
he should doe so no more but presently one of Lankaster cominge
to his Masters hous he went with him to the ordenary and came not
whom till the day after. . . . The first of March his Master went to
the bay and gave him great Charge to stay at whom and Looke

[64] Middlesex Files, folder 23, group 3 (1660).

Carfully to his business but he went away at his owne pleasur and Came whome in the night and broke the doare of the hinges: and tenn days after his master sent him to cut a tree which was not above on houres warke and he came not whome tell the Next day.[65]

Servants could frequently find time for fun when their master was absent upon business. Sometimes on such occasions they went on a spree at his expense. The story of one forbidden feast came out in court when

John Befer, upon examination, said that he knew of the killing of his mistress' pigs and that Stephen and George killed and dressed the flesh but he did not help them. He was in the council, however, and partook in eating thereof. Also that John Palmer and Stephen killed the second hog and helped make the fire for it, that Stephen suggested to him breaking into the room wherein the house provisions were put under lock and key, that after Stephen had loosened the board, he helped to pull it up and himself, Stephen and Palmer went down and took cider, strong beer, pastry and cheese and all three of them went down several times through the place opened, and took sugar, plums, marmulet and butter. Also that Palmer, by putting his arm into a locked cubbard by means of a pin loose in the ledge, took out the key of the cellar. That there was some linen used, but what was washed and returned he did not know, yet he thought that one napkin was brought to be washed, and that he and Palmer did take powder and shot. That it was a usual thing to seek for and take the eggs from the family for themselves.[66]

Even when the master of the house was at home, servants managed to get more free time than they were entitled to. They might be kept on the job all day, but it was easy to slip away at night to the nearest tavern. Here, in spite of the laws forbidding their admission, they were likely to find congenial company. The numerous indictments against tavernkeepers and others for breaking the laws[67] show that servants squandered over cakes and ale much of

---

[65] Ibid., folder 53, group 4 (1669).
[66] *Essex Court Records*, III, 144.
[67] E.g., *Essex Court Records*, II, 180; IV, 237, 275; V, 143.

the time which they should have spent resting for the morrow's labor. Most of them were able to get a little spending money for these luxuries, whether from wages, theft, or tips—for it was already a custom in the seventeenth century for guests or lodgers in a house to tip the servants when they left.[68]

At night, too, servants found time for love affairs. Most servants who lived with their masters were unmarried.[69] Apprentices had, of course, agreed by contract not to marry, but neither an apprentice nor any other servant would normally have been able to support both a wife and a master anyhow. Indentured servants and servants who were working off a debt[70] or a criminal sentence received no wages, and a hired servant who lived with his master had probably not yet earned enough to set up for himself. As soon as he did, he would marry and move out. Slaves, since they could not look forward to independence, were sometimes allowed to marry because they could not otherwise have had lawful outlet for the lust which Puritans recognized as a universal human frailty.[71] But by and large servants must have been unmarried, so that if they satisfied their sexual desires at all, they did so illegally.

It was not difficult to find opportunities under cover of darkness. Solomon Phipps's Negro man confessed on May 16, 1682, that the

---

[68] The members of the Essex County Court regularly voted tips to the servants who attended them in the house where they sat, and in one case tried before the court a mistress testified concerning her maid servant that "as for money shee had of lodgers at my house, she layd it out so needlessly that I have blamed her for it" (*Essex Court Records*, VII, 44).

[69] Occasionally, however, a married couple did live with and serve the same master, as is evidenced by the judgment requiring John Tibb to serve his master a quarter of a year longer than his term of indenture "for his wife running awaye and charges his master was put to thereby" (*Essex Court Records*, V, 23).

[70] Of course, a married man might be delivered as a servant to his creditor. In 1678 Edward Winter, a married man, was made servant to Edmund Batter for five years in order to satisfy a debt, with the provision that Batter should keep only one-third of his earnings; the other two-thirds was to go to his family (*Essex Court Records*, VII, 153).

[71] On this subject see George E. Howard, *A History of Matrimonial Institutions* (Chicago and London, 1904), II, 215–226.

week before, at night, he had broken into the house of Lawrence Hammond in Charlestown and visited the Negro maid in the garrett "and that the like he hath done at severall other times before."[72] Joshua Fletcher acknowledged in court "that three severall nights, after bedtime, he went into Mr. Fiskes Dwelling house at Chelmsford, at an open window by a ladder that he brought with him. the said window opening into a chamber, where was the lodging place of Gresill Juell servant to mr. Fiske."[73] In fine weather it was not necessary to search out a maid in her bedroom. Rachel Smith was seduced in an open field, by a man whom she did not even know, who "gave her strong liquors, and told her that it was not the first time he had been with maydes after his master was in bed."[74] Often it was not even necessary for a servant to go out of the house. Frequently men and women servants slept in the same room;[75] and since it seems to have been the custom to sleep without nightclothes,[76] temptation was always at hand. Many love affairs

[72] Middlesex Files, folder 99, group 3.

[73] Ibid., folder 47, group 3.

[74] Ibid., folder 44, group 3.

[75] See, for example, the testimony of Elizabeth Fowler against Hannah Gray (*Essex Court Records*, V, 290, March 1674), that Hannah "was a lying girl, and several times in the night when deponent waked, she missed her and heard her laughing and giggling at the boys' bed which was in the same room."

[76] Such at least is the inference I draw from the following deposition in the files of the Middlesex County Court (my italics): "Benjamin Chamberlene aged about 21 years doth testifie that on the 30th of September last. Joseph Graves was at the house of Thomas Goble in concord. in the night time. and tarrying there after the said Thomas Goble was in bed, who lay in the same roome, and also two mayds in another bed. viz: Ester Necholls and Mary Goble. the said Joseph Graves went and set by the bedside and talked with them privately and after that sung some short songs to them. and after a while I saw the said Joseph Graves in bed with them. — the cloathes were over him. The said mayds as he apprehends being *in their naked beds* . . ." (folder 62, group 6). Cf. Thomas Tusser, *Five Hundred Points of Good Husbandry* (edition of London, 1931), p. 162:

> *The first cock croweth.*
> Past five a clock, Holla: maid sleeping beware
> *The next cock croweth.*
> Least quickly your Mistress uncover your bare.
> *Maides, up I beeseech yee,*

between servants must have had their consummation in a crowded bedroom, even on a bed in which other people were sleeping.

The punishment for fornication was left largely to the discretion of the court. The law provided that the judges could enjoin marriage, fine, or corporal punishment as they saw fit.[77] In practice a fine or a whipping was the normal sentence, but in addition the law required the reputed father of an illegitimate child to pay for its support and education.[78] The reputed father, according to statute, was the person whom the mother accused when questioned in her labor. The law probably acted as the opposite of a deterrent, for by means of it an innocent but wealthy person could be made to pay for the child of a penniless servant. For example, when Elizabeth Wells bore a child, she laid it to James Tufts, her master's son. Goodman Tufts affirmed that Andrew Robinson, servant to Goodman Dexter, was the real father of the child, and he brought the following testimony as evidence:

Wee Elizabeth Jefts aged 15 ears and Mary tufts aged 14 ears doe testyfie that their being one at our hous sumtime the last winter who sayed that thear was a new law made Concerning bastards that If aney man wear aqused with a bastard and the woman which had aqused him did stand unto it in her labor that he should bee the reputed father of it and should mayntaine it Elizabeth Wells hearing of the sayd law she sayed unto us that If shee should bee with child shee would bee sure to lay it un to won who was rich enough abell to mayntayne it wheather it wear his or no and shee farder sayed Elizabeth Jefts would not you doe so likewise If it weare your case and I sayed no by no means for right must tacke place: and the sayd Elizabeth wells sayed If it wear my Caus I think I should doe soe.[79]

A tragic, unsigned letter that somehow found its way into the Mid-

---

Least Mistres doe breech yee:
To worke and away,
As fast as ye may.
[77] *Massachusetts Laws of 1648*, p. 23.
[78] *Massachusetts Laws of 1672*, p. 55.
[79] Middlesex Files, folder 52, group 2.

dlesex County Court files gives more direct evidence of the practice
which Elizabeth Wells professed.

der loue i remember my loue to you hoping your welfar and i hop
to imbras the but now i rit to you to let you nowe that i am a child
by you and i wil ether kil it or lay it to an other and you shal
have no blame at al for I haue had many children and none [of
their fathers?] have none of them. . . .[80]

If a servant had to undertake the support of his child, it meant
that his master paid the bills and that the servant worked for a
longer term. The expense, however, was only about three shillings
a week,[81] and owing to the high value of labor, the child might be
put off to a master at a very early age. In return for bringing it up,
the master got its services until it reached twenty-one. The Essex
Court recorded on November 6, 1678, that "Richard Woolery being
the reputed father of the child of Abigaill Morse, the child Hanah
Woolery, being now two years and seven weeks old, was bound to
Joseph Pike until twenty-one years of age. Said Woolery was discharged from paying any more."[82]

Thus in spite of every disadvantage some servants did manage to
have a "private life," illegal though it was.

On the other hand, dutiful servants, who restrained themselves
and waited patiently for the end of their service, could console
themselves with the fact that they would probably win independence more quickly than the profligates who wasted their masters'
time with maids and boon companions. Puritan justice demanded
that when servants had been "unfaithfull, negligent, or unprofitable
in their service, notwithstanding the good usage of their Masters,
they shall not be dismissed till they have made satisfaction according to the judgement of Authoritie."[83] Satisfaction inevitably consisted of further service without compensation.

When a servant had once become free of his master, the path to

---

[80] Ibid., folder 30, group 4.
[81] See *Essex Court Records*, II, 68, 372, 384; V, 410–411; VII, 187, 315,
410; VIII, 12–13, 219, 299, 345, 383.
[82] *Essex Court Records*, VII, 97.
[83] *Massachusetts Laws of 1648*, p. 39.

prosperity was a short one. Patience and industry brought quick results when applied to the forests, the oceans, and the virgin soil of the new world. Edward Johnson observed in 1654 that there were "many hundreds of labouring men, who had not enough to bring them over, yet now worth scores, and some hundreds of pounds."[84] An example was Samuel Haines, who came to New England as a servant in 1635 and later became a selectman of Portsmouth, New Hampshire, and deacon of the First Church there.[85] The fact that a man had once been a servant did not weigh heavily against him in the social scale, because many Puritans of the most respectable families had undergone some kind of servitude in their youth either as apprentices or as hired servants. Wealthy and aristocratic parents showed no hesitation in making their children servants to their friends or even to strangers. Emmanuel Downing's son served John Winthrop, Jr., while John's brother Samuel served a Spanish merchant in Barbados; and Samuel Sewall reflected pleasantly in his old age that whereas his sister had once served Madam Usher, the latter's grandchildren were now serving him.[86]

These facts help to brighten the picture of New England servitude. The non-Puritan servant might chafe under the restrictions imposed upon him by the godly rulers of New England, but he had as companions in his condition the children of men who were equal in rank to his master. Servitude in New England was not simply a device by which one class of men got work out of another class. It was also a school, where vocational training was combined with discipline in good manners and guidance in religion, a school of which all servants were the pupils and to which many respectable and godly men sent their children.

[84] Edward Johnson, *Wonder-Working Providence of Sions Savior in New England* (Andover, 1867), p. 175.
[85] *New England Historical and Genealogical Register*, XXIII, 150–153.
[86] Massachusetts Historical Society *Collections*, fourth series, VI, 40b–40c; fifth series, VIII, 202–203; sixth series, II, 204.

VI

The Family in the Social Order

*I*F MEN had only behaved themselves in the beginning, they would never have needed such complicated things as churches and civil governments. This was the first premise of Puritan political and social thought. In the Garden of Eden, which was the world as God had originally planned it, men lived innocently and happily with no need for any social organization apart from that provided by the family. It was only after Adam and Eve had tasted the forbidden fruit that need arose for stronger organizations. The family in itself was insufficient to cope with the awakened evil of human nature. After expelling man from Paradise, therefore, God arranged for the establishment of churches and states.

In creating these institutions, God did not abolish the family, nor did he set up a new order of things out of whole cloth. Instead he developed churches and states out of the family, which continued to be, in the Puritans' opinion, "the very *First Society* that by the Direction and Providence of GOD, is produced among the Children of Men."[1] God's procedure in this instance, as in all instances, was deliberate: it expressed the importance which he attached to the family. If he had chosen to, he could have created at one stroke *"millions of people, who might presently have constituted civill states and Churches also: but he chose rather, to lay the foundations both of State and Church, in a family, making that the Mother Hive, out of which both those swarms of State and Church,*

[1] Cotton Mather, *Family Religion Urged* (Boston, 1709), p. 1.

133

issued forth."[2] The state existed in embryo in the authority which
God gave Adam over his family, an authority which was later
explicitly stated in the fifth commandment. The church had its
prototype in the simple adoration which Adam and Eve offered to
their maker. What then was the purpose of church and state, and
what was their relationship to the family, the "Mother Hive" from
which they had issued?

The church was established on earth in order to restore the
proper harmony between man and his maker. After the fall from
grace, man was incapable of communicating directly with God. He
needed some intermediary; he needed, in other words, the Church
of Christ. Although Christ himself did not appear until thousands
of years later, the first Christian church, the Puritans argued, was
the family of Abraham. The church thus continued to be for some
time after the fall a purely domestic institution. Soon, however,
God extended the church to the whole tribe of Israel and, after
Christ's incarnation, to all believers who joined themselves together
for the purpose of worship. When Christ should come for a second
time, the church would undergo another transformation; until then
it would remain in the "congregational" form. So, at least, the
Puritans reasoned, and they called themselves "Congregationalists"
accordingly.

A congregational church was simply a group of individuals joined
together by voluntary agreement for the purpose of worship. Not
everyone could join, for according to Puritan interpretation of the
Bible a church was not an inclusive organization embracing all
the people of a country or a neighborhood. Rather it was an association of saints, of men and women whose belief in Christ was
produced not by their own feeble efforts of will but by the operation
of the Holy Spirit on their souls. A saint could point to his conversion, when the Spirit came to him, and before being admitted to
a church he would have to describe the experience in some detail
to the other members, in order to presuade them that he was, in
truth, a saint.

[2] Cobbett, *Fruitfull and Usefull Discourse*, sig. A3.

The whole procedure was voluntary. Anyone who could demonstrate his conversion was qualified for admission, but no one could compel him to join, nor could any church be compelled by higher authority to accept him. As John Davenport put it, "Both parties, before, were free, the one, to offer himself into fellowship, or not; the other, to admit him, or not. If such joyn together it is by their free consent, and must be by mutual engagement."[3]

In spite of its congregational form, however, the Puritan church showed signs of its domestic origin, for it included not only individual believers but the children of believers as well. When a man or woman joined it voluntarily, his or her offspring entered automatically without opportunity for a "free consent." All minor children, whether living or yet to be born, were included in the agreement of their parents. After they had grown to maturity they had to renew the agreement for themselves, but as long as they remained under parental care, they enjoyed the privileges of their parents' membership. The Puritans thus composed their churches of families rather than individuals. They justified the practice by reference to the origin of the church in the family of Abraham. God's covenant with Abraham, they said, had included Abraham's family. Surely God would be no less liberal now. "The faith of the parent," John Cotton explained, "doth bring the Children and houshold of a Christian, even now in the days of the new Testament, under a Covenant of salvation, as well as the faith of *Abraham* brought his houshold of old under the same covenant."[4]

Though children were admitted to church membership on the strength of their parents' covenant, there was some controversy about the rest of the household. John Davenport wished to exclude it,[5] John Cotton to admit it. Cotton insisted that the covenant ex-

---

[3] John Davenport, *The power of Congregational Churches Asserted and Vindicated* (London, 1672), p. 39.

[4] John Cotton, *The Grounds and Ends of the Baptisme of the Children of the Faithfull* (London, 1647), p. 48.

[5] See John Davenport, *Letters*, pp. 262–266; Increase Mather, *A Disputation concerning Church Members and their Children* (London, 1659), p. 19: "Adopted children and Infant-servants, regularly and absolutely subjected to

tended to all the children of the house whether natural or adopted and also to all servants. In *The Covenant of Gods Free Grace* he flatly stated that "the Covenant is made to the housholders and their servants,"[6] and he supported his assertion by pointing out elsewhere that Abraham's household included "not onely his sonnes, but also all that were borne in his house, or bought with his money."[7] Though Cotton was the most revered of New England ministers and though his opinion doubtless carried great weight, there is no evidence that servants received any ecclesiastical privileges because of their master's connection with a church. This lack of evidence may be due to the fragmentary character of seventeenth-century church records; but whatever their attitude toward the other members of a household, all orthodox New England churches acknowledged that children should partake in their parents' membership. The Puritans, in other words, thought of their church as an organization made up of families rather than individuals.

If the church showed its domestic origin by including children with their parents, the family gave signs of its former ecclesiastical activities by conducting regular religious devotions. Though the church had undertaken public organization of religious instruction and worship, the family continued to perform these functions privately. Every morning immediately upon rising and every evening before retiring a good Puritan father led his household in prayer, in scriptural reading, and in singing of psalms. Whenever they sat down at table together, he offered thanks to the Lord.[8]

---

the Government and dispose of such heads of Families as are in Church-covenant, though they cannot be said to be their natural seed, yet in regard the Scriptures (according to the judgment of many Godly Learned) extend to them the same Covenant priviledges with their Natural seed, we judge not any Churches who are like-minded with them, for their practice herein: All which notwithstanding, yet we desire at present to leave this question without all prejudice on our parts to after free disquisition."

[6] P. 19.

[7] John Cotton, *Grounds and Ends*, p. 188.

[8] Thomas Cobbett, *A Practical Discourse of Prayer* (London, 1654), pp. 103–104; Deodat Lawson, *The Duty and Property of a Religious Housholder*, pp. 23–26; Cotton Mather, *A Family-Sacrifice*, pp. 27–28, 30–34.

None of these devotons was supposed to be long. Although the Puritans enjoyed two-hour sermons on the Sabbath, they tried to avoid prolixity in their family services. Cotton Mather says of John Cotton that he always read a chapter of Scripture to his family every morning and every evening, "with a little applicatory exposition, before and after which he made a prayer; but he was very short in all, accounting as Mr. Dod, Mr. Bains, and other great saints did before him, 'That it was a thing inconvenient many ways to be tedious in family duties.' "[9]

Sewall's diary is filled with references to the performance of these family duties, such as: "Begun in Course to read the New-Testament, having ended the Revelation the night before," or "Read the 16th of the first Chron. in the family"; or "125th Psalm Sung by us in course in the family". During a voyage to England he frequently made such entries as "In the even reef of the Main-sail. I read the 74th Psalm, being that I should have read at home in the family."[10] The diary also shows that Sewall made a practice of having his children take an active part in family devotions, both in prayer and in biblical readings. On January 10, 1689, he wrote: "It falls to my Daughter Elisabeth's Share to read the 24. of Isaiah, which she doth with many Tears not being very well, and the Contents of the Chapter, and Sympathy with her draw Tears from me also."[11] Seven years later Betty experienced further religious fears: "Sabbath, May 3, 1696. Betty can hardly read her chapter for weeping; tells me she is afraid she is gon back, does not taste that sweetness in reading the Word which once she did; fears that what was once upon her is worn off. I said what I could to her, and in the evening pray'd with her alone."[12] Sewall was always very sympathetic with his children in their religious trials, trials which were frequently brought on by his own endeavors to awaken them. Just two days after Betty's tears over the 24th of Isaiah, he brought young Sam to a similar state of fear and trembling:

[9] Cotton Mather, *Magnalia*, I, 277–278.
[10] Sewall, "Diary," I, 113, 120, 237.
[11] Ibid., I, 308.
[12] Ibid., I, 423.

Sabbath, Jan. 12. Richard Dummer, a flourishing youth of 9 years old, dies of the Small Pocks. I tell Sam. of it and what need he had to prepare for Death, and therefore to endeavour really to pray when he said over the Lord's Prayer: He seem'd not much to mind, eating an Apple; but when he came to say, Our father, he burst out into a bitter Cry, and when I askt what was the matter and he could speak, he burst out into a bitter Cry and said he was afraid he should die. I pray'd with him, and read Scriptures comforting against death, as, O death where is thy sting, &c. All things yours. Life and Immortality brought to light by Christ, &c. 'Twas at noon.[13]

Cotton Mather also gave his personal attention to his children's religious welfare:

7d. 9m. [November.] Lords-Day. I took my little Daughter, Katy, into my Study; and there I told my Child, that I am to dy shortly, and shee must, when I am Dead, Remember every Thing, that I said unto her.

I sett before her, the sinful and woful Condition of her Nature, and I charg'd her, to pray in secret Places, every Day, without ceasing, that God for the Sake of Jesus Christ would give her a New Heart, and pardon Her Sins, and make her a Servant of His.

I gave her to understand, that when I am taken from her, shee must look to meet with more humbling Afflictions than shee does, now shee has a careful and a tender Father to provide for her; but, if shee would pray constantly, God in the Lord Jesus Christ, would bee a Father to her, and make all Afflictions work together for her Good.

I signified unto her, That the People of God, would much observe how shee carried herself, and that I had written a Book, about, Ungodly Children, in the Conclusion whereof I say, that this Book will bee a terrible Witness against my own Children, if any of them should not bee Godly.

At length, with many Tears, both on my Part, and hers, I told my Child, that God had from Heaven assured mee, and the good Angels of God had satisfied mee, that shee shall bee brought Home

---

[13] Ibid., I, 308–309.

unto the Lord Jesus Christ, and bee one of His forever. I bid her use this, as an Encouragement unto her Supplications unto the Lord, for His Grace. But I therwithal told her, that if shee did not now, in her Childhood seek the Lord, and give herself up unto Him, some dreadful Afflictions must befal her, that so her Father's Faith may come at its Accomplishments.

I thereupon made the Child kneel down by mee; and I poured out my Cries unto the Lord, that Hee would lay His Hands upon her, and bless her and save her, and make her a *Temple* of His Glory. It will bee so; It will be so!

I write this, the more particularly, that the Child may hereafter have the Benefit of reading it.[14]

This type of domestic instruction and worship was considered indispensable to the success of the weekly services in the church, for religion was too important a matter to be left to weekly lessons. If the family failed to teach its members properly, neither the state nor the church could be expected to accomplish much. As Wadsworth put it:

Without *Family care* the labour of Magistrates and Ministers for Reformation and Propagating Religion, is likely to be in a great measure unsuccessful. It's much to be fear'd, Young Persons wont much mind what's said by Ministers in Publick, if they are not Instructed at home: nor will they much regard good Laws made by Civil Authority, if they are not well counsel'd and govern'd at home.[15]

The church, therefore, was careful to encourage the performance of family religious duties. The ministers were constantly reiterating the point. Samuel Willard affirmed in 1677 that the church must "looke to all the families that they maintaine family worship and instruction."[16] In 1659 Increase Mather, as spokesman for a convention of Boston ministers, wrote that "it is the Duty of the Elders and Church to call upon Parents to bring up their children in the

[14] Cotton Mather, "Diary," I, 239–240.
[15] Wadsworth, *Well-Ordered Family*, p. 84.
[16] Boston Sermons, Oct. 14, 1677.

nurture and admonition of the Lord, and to see as much as in them
lieth, that it be effectually done."[17] Twenty-one years later Mather's church in Boston announced:

We promise (by the help of Christ) that we will endeavour to
walk before God in our houses, with a perfect heart; and that we
will uphold the worship of God therein continually, according as
he in his word doth require, both in respect of Prayer, and reading
the Scriptures, that so the word of Christ may dwell richly in us;
And that we will do what in us lyeth, to bring up our children for
Christ, that they may become such, as they that have the Lords
name put upon them by a solemn dedication to God in Christ,
ought to be; and that therefore we will (so far as there shall be
need of it) Catechize them, and exhort and charge them to fear and
serve the Lord, and endeavour to set an holy Example before them,
and be much in prayer for their Conversion and Salvation.[18]

The church at Dorchester promised in 1677,

to Reforme our famelys, Engageing our selves to a Conscientious
Care to set up and maintaine the Worship of god in them and to
walk in our houses with perfect harts in a faithfull discharge of all
Domestick dutys: Educating Instructing and Charging our Children and our households, to keepe the ways of the lord; Restraining
them as much as in us lyeth, from all evil and especially the Sins of
the times and watching over them in the lord.[19]

Without making such an explicit engagement the First Church of
Boston voted unanimously in December 1669, "that the Elders
should go from hows to howse to visit the familys and see how
they are instructed in the grounds of religion."[20]
Maintenance of family religion and instruction was not the only
domestic duty which the church supervised. Since the compact by

[17] Increase Mather, *A Disputation concerning Church-Members and their
Children*, p. 14.
[18] Increase Mather, *Returning unto God the Great Concernment* (Boston,
1680), p. 20.
[19] *Records of the First Church in Dorchester* (Boston, 1891), p. 19.
[20] Colonial Society of Massachusetts *Publications*, XXXIX, 64.

which it was formed always included a promise by the members to "walk together" in obedience to God, the church had as much interest as the state in enforcing the other laws of God, including the laws which governed domestic relations. Its means of enforcement, however, differed from the state's in being entirely spiritual: censure, admonition, and excommunication were its only weapons. The records indicate that these weapons were freely used to reform family disorders. The First Church of Boston excommunicated Mary Wharton "for her reviling of her husband and stricking of him and other vild and wicked Courses," and Mercy Verin "for uncivill Carriage with Samuel Smith and bad Language to her husband."[21] It gave the same treatment to John Webb "for his attempt of uncleanes and withdrawing from his wif and his impenitence after all"[22] and to James Mattock for a number of marital offenses, including the fact "that he denyed Coniugall fellowship unto his wife for the space of 2 years together upon pretence of taking Revenge upon himself for his abusing of her before marryage."[23] It cast out William Franklin "for Rygarous and Cruell Correction of his servants, and for sundry lyes in his being dealt withall about it, both pryvately and publiquely."[24] It admonished Temperance Sweete "for having received to house and given entertainment unto disorderly Company and ministring unto them wine and strong waters even unto Drunkennesse and that not without some iniquity both in the measure and pryce thereof."[25] Other churches took similar action. The Dorchester church admonished Robert Spur for "giveing entertainement in his hous of loos and vaine persons espesally Joseph Belcher his frequent Coming to his daughter Contrary to the admonition of the Court which was greatly to the offence of the said Belchers neerest relations and divers others."[26] The Roxbury church admonished "sister Cleaves," "for unseason-

[21] Ibid., pp. 62, 70.
[22] Ibid., p. 61.
[23] Ibid., pp. 26–27.
[24] Ibid., p. 44.
[25] Ibid., p. 28.
[26] *Records of the First Church in Dorchester*, p. 70; see also p. 84.

able entertaining and corrupting other folks servants and children."[27] The list could go on much longer. Though seventeenth-century church records are few and sadly incomplete in detail, they do reveal clearly that most churches punished breaches of family order.

The church's sphere of operation, however, was limited: obviously it could not excommunicate anyone who did not belong to it, and admonition and censure would certainly not bother ungodly persons anyhow. Evidently a further authority was necessary. The state provided it.

Civil government, the Puritans believed, became an absolute necessity after the fall of man. The sin of the first Adam had so vitiated human nature that family governors could not be trusted to maintain the order that God had commanded. They might control their children and servants, but who was to control them? Who was to settle the quarrels into which their degenerate natures would lead them? Furthermore, if some one committed a crime deserving of death, who was to inflict the punishment? God had given family governors no power of life and death. Clearly a superior authority was called for. A group of families, "not having compleat Government within themselves, must combine in a Commonwealth."[28] Just as servitude was introduced after the fall of man to help restrain human corruption, for the same reason the civil state, unnecessary in Eden, became essential in a degenerate world. It was "a relief for the Children of men, against the mischief which would otherwise devour them."[29] A civil government was necessary because family government was now inadequate to enforce the laws of God.

Civil government, once established, did not supersede the family as a means of enforcing the laws of God. The state made no demand that the heads of families should "yield up their Family-

[27] *A Report of the Record Commissioners, containing the Roxbury Land and Church Records* (the sixth report of the Boston Record Commissioners, Boston, 1881), p. 95.

[28] Davenport, *Power of Congregational Churches*, pp. 130–131.

[29] Samuel Willard, *The Character of a Good Ruler* (Boston, 1694), p. 3.

Government over their Wives, Children, and Servants, respectively, to rule them in common with other Masters of Families."[30] Rather it gave additional support to their authority, because without assistance from them it could not have begun to accomplish its task of enforcing the laws of God. Those laws, as the Puritans interpreted them, covered the minutest details of personal action. They forbade work on the Sabbath and idleness on weekdays; they forbade blasphemy, lying, idolatry, and heresy. They forbade "excessive wages" and "unreasonable prizes"; they forbade usury, tippling, and the playing of shuffleboard.[31] Even a multitude of petty officers would not have provided the close supervision of every individual that an effective enforcement of such prohibitions required, but family governors could provide it. The chief problem for the state, therefore, was to see that family governors did their duty.

The Puritans recognized this fact in characterizing families as "the root whence church and Commonwealth Cometh,"[32] "the Seminaries of Church and Common-wealth,"[33] "the foundation of all societies,"[34] and "the *Nurseries* of all Societies."[35] "*Well-ordered Families*," Cotton Mather explained, "naturally produce a *Good Order* in other *Societies*. When *Families* are under an *Ill Discipline*, all other *Societies* being therefore *Ill Disciplined*, will feel that Error in the *First* Concoction."[36] "Such as Families are," James Fitch warned, "such at last the Church and Common-wealth must be."[37] If these statements were platitudinous, they nevertheless expressed the assumption upon which Puritan leaders acted, namely that the state is made up of families rather than individ-

---

[30] Davenport, *Power of Congregational Churches*, p. 131.

[31] *Massachusetts Laws of 1672*, pp. 14, 57, 58–63, 66, 80–85, 91–92, 120, 132–134, 153.

[32] Boston Sermons, January 14, 1671–2.

[33] Eleazar Mather, *A Serious Exhortation*, p. 20.

[34] Samuel Hooker, *Righteousness Rained from Heaven* (Cambridge, 1677), p. 25.

[35] Cotton Mather, *A Family Well-Ordered* (Boston, 1699), p. 3.

[36] Loc. cit.

[37] James Fitch, *An Explanation of the Solemn Advice* (Boston, 1683), p. 15.

uals.[38] The governors of the Massachusetts Bay Company, for example, tried from the very outset to bring every member of their colony who was not himself the head of a family under the control of family government. This policy was not easily put into practice during the early stages of the enterprise, for the first settlers sent over after the organization of the company were a group of male servants, under the direction of a deputy governor, John Endicott. Since no natural families could exist in such a group, the only way to obtain the benefits of domestic discipline was to establish artificial families. On April 21, 1629, the company wrote Endicott a letter containing the following instructions:

For the better accomodation of businesses, wee have devyded the servants belonging to the Company into severall famylies, as wee desire and intend they should live togeather; a coppy wherof wee send yow heere inclosed, that yow may accordingly appoint each man his charge and dutie. . . . Our earnest desire is, that you take spetiall care, in setlinge these ffamilies, that the cheife in the familie (at least some of them) bee grounded in religion; wherby morning and evening famylie dutyes may bee duely performed, and a watchfull eye held over all in each familie by one or more in each famylie to bee appointed thereto, that soe disorders may bee prevented, and ill weeds nipt before they take too great a head. It wilbe a business worthy your best endeavours to looke unto this in the beginninge, and if neede bee, to make some exemplary to all the rest; otherwise your government wilbe esteemed as a scar crowe.[39]

After the Great Migration had brought twenty thousand Englishmen to the new world, such makeshift families were no longer

---

[38] John Winthrop thought that a commonwealth resulted from "many familyes subjecting themselves to rulers and laws" (Thomas Hutchinson, ed., *A Collection of Original Papers Relative to the History of the Colony of Massachusetts-Bay* [Boston, 1769], p. 67). John Eliot, in describing the social compact by which his ideal Christian state was to be inaugurated, wrote that "the Child is implicitely comprehended in the Fathers Covenant, the Wife is explicitely comprehended in her Husbands" (John Eliot, *The Christian Commonwealth: or, The Civil Policy of the Rising Kingdom of Jesus Christ* [London, 1659], p. 3.)

[39] *Massachusetts Records*, I, 397.

necessary, for fortunately the migration to New England, unlike that to Virginia, was primarily one of families. So at least the passenger lists seem to indicate.[40] The rulers of the various New England colonies took advantage of this influx of families to place all stray bachelors and maids under the discipline of a real family governor. In 1638 Massachusetts ordered every town to "dispose of all single persons and inmates within their towne to servise, or otherwise."[41] In February 1636/7 Connecticut provided "that noe yonge man that is neither maried nor hath any servaunte, and be noe publicke officer, shall keepe howse by himself, without consent of the Towne where he lives first had, under paine of 20s. per weeke."[42] Plymouth enacted similar legisation in 1669:

Wheras great Inconvenience hath arisen by single persons in this Collonie being for themselves and not betakeing themselves to live in well Governed famillies It is enacted by the Court that henceforth noe single person be suffered to live of himselfe or in any family but such as the Celectmen of the Towne shall approve of; and if any person or persons shall refuse or neglect to attend such order as shalbe given them by the Celectmen; That such person or persons shalbe sumoned to the Court to be proceeded with as the matter shall require.[43]

The purpose of all this legislation is clearly explained by the judgment of the Essex County Court in a particular case:

Court being informed that John Littleale of Haverhill lay in a house by himself contrary to the law of the country, whereby he is subject to much sin and iniquity, which ordinarily are the companions and consequences of a solitary life, it was ordered Oct. 12,

[40] For example, of 206 persons who settled in Hingham between 1633 and 1639, only 10 came by themselves as single men or women. The rest were divided among 38 families (*New England Historical and Genealogical Register*, XV, 25–27). Other available records tell the same story. See the lists printed in Charles E. Banks, *The Planters of the Commonwealth* (Boston, 1930).

[41] *Massachusetts Records*, I, 186 (Dec. 13, 1636).

[42] *Connecticut Records*, I, 8 (Feb. 21, 1636/7).

[43] *Plymouth Records*, XI, 223.

1672, that within six weeks after date he remove and settle himself in some orderly family in the town, and be subject to the orderly rules of family government, unless he remove from the town within that time. If he did not comply with this order, the selectmen were ordered to place him in some family, which if he refused, a warrant was to be issued to place him in the house of correction at Hampton.[44]

The enforcement of the laws against single persons was usually left to the selectmen of the various towns. Occasionally, however, the county courts would send instructions, specially printed for this purpose, enjoining the selectmen to do their duty. The Middlesex County Court sent such instructions to the towns under its jurisdiction in October 1668. Thirty-two offenders were reported, many of whom later recorded in court that they had made arrangements to live in a family.[45] In April 1680 the court made another drive against single persons, but the five towns whose returns have been preserved reported that there were no offenders within their precincts.[46]

Having taken such care to bring everyone under the authority of a family ruler, the state did its utmost to support such rulers in the proper exercise of their authority. We have already noticed the strict punishments it provided for disobedient children and servants. It also protected family governors from outsiders who might undermine their power. For example, it fined Nicholas Russell "for remaining in Nicholas Penyon's house after he had ordered him to keep away, being jealous of his wife."[47] It punished tavern keepers and anyone else who entertained children or servants without the consent of their parents or masters.[48] Invariably it took favorable action upon petitions like the following:

To the Honourable County Court, now seting in Cambridge:

[44] *Essex Court Records*, V, 104.
[45] Middlesex Files, folder 49, group 4; folder 51, groups 4 and 5.
[46] Ibid., folder 88, group 6.
[47] *Essex Court Records*, I, 134 (February, 1648).
[48] Ibid., II, 180; IV, 237, 275; V, 143; and *Suffolk Court Records*, p. 336.

Wee whose names are under written, present this our Humble petition; and that in obedience to both the Laws of God, and Man, that the Honoured Court now seting would please to take some speedy course, [toward] the reforming and reclaiming of the Familyes, of John Allen, and of his son; as to those ungodly wicked unchristian practices of a frequent entertaining of Servants, of their neighbours especially the House of John Allin, where such are entertained, not only for a few houres, but almost daily some-tims; and that to the great griefe of thir Masters; and especially such servants, are (by such a wicked practice) debauched, made Idle wanton discontented; and thir masters greatly wronged; and above all, the name of God, and Intrust of Religion greatly suffers, by such wicked and vile practices.[49]

Since it relied so heavily upon the family, the state took care to see that family rulers were worthy of their responsibilities. Men like John Allin obviously did not deserve to have charge of a family, and the courts frequently prevented such persons from setting up households or even deprived them of their households after they were set up. The General Court of Plymouth provided in 1636

that none bee alowed to bee housekeepers or build any Cottages or dwelling houses till such time as they bee allowed by the Governor and Councell of Assistants or some one or more of them and that this order bee strictly observed; . . . that noe servant coming out of England or elswhere; and is to serve a master for some time bee admited to bee for himselfe; untill he have served out his time either with his master or some other; although hee shall buy out his time; except hee have bin an houskeeper or master of a family or meet or fitt to bee soe.[50]

Although the other colonies had no similar legislation on the sub-ject, they nevertheless took drastic action against anyone whom they considered unfit for the duties of a parent or master. When Captain James Johnson of Boston was "complained of for dis-

[49] Middlesex Files, folder 114, group 3.
[50] *Plymouth Records*, XI, 191.

orderly carriages in his Family, giving entertainment to persons at unseasonable houres of the night and other misdemeanors," the Suffolk County Court ordered "the said Captain Johnson to breake up housekeeping and to dispose of himselfe into some good orderly Family within one Fortnight next following or that then the Select-men of Boston take care to dispose of him as above-said."[51] Anyone who had shown himself to be an habitual sinner was not qualified to bring up children. When Robert Styles of Dorchester was pre-sented "for not attending the publique worship of God, negligence in his calling and not Submitting to Authority," he was ordered to "put forth his Children, or otherwise the Select men are hereby impoured to do it according to Law."[52] The selectmen of every town regularly inspected families to see that parents fulfilled their educational duties.[53] Whatever their other merits, parents found negligent in this respect might have their children taken from them and placed with someone more worthy. William Scant of Braintree was brought before the Suffolk Court for

not ordering and disposeing of his Children as may bee for theire good education and for refuseing to consent to the Selectmen of Brantery in the putting of them forth to Service as the law directs. The Court having duely weighed and considered what was alleaged by him and the State of his Family doe leave it to the prudence of the Selectmen of Brantery to dispose of his Children to Service so far forth as the necessity of his Family will give leave.[54]

As the settlements grew, it became more and more difficult for the selectmen and constables to supervise the government of all the families in their towns. Consequently in the years from 1675 to 1679 Massachusetts established a new group of officers for the pur-pose of inspecting and re-enforcing family government. These officers, known as tithingmen, were empowered in 1675 to enforce a law against drunkenness. The law provided that

[51] *Suffolk Court Records*, pp. 646–647 (Nov. 23, 1675).
[52] Ibid., p. 915.
[53] E.g., *Watertown Records* (Watertown, 1894), I, 102–105, 107, 109, 113, 121, 122, 128, 135, 137, 145.
[54] *Suffolk Court Records*, p. 599.

the Select men of every Town shall choose some sober and discreet persons to be Authorized from the County Court, each of whom shall take the Charge of *Ten* or *Twelve Families* of his Neighbour-hood, and shall diligently inspect them, and present the names of such persons so transgressing to the Magistrate, Commissioner, or Select men of the Town, who shall return the same to be proceeded with by the next County Court, as the law directs.[55]

In May 1677 the tithingmen received power to apprehend and ar-rest "all Sabbath-breakers and disorderly Tiplers, or such as keep Licensed Houses, or others that shall suffer any disorder in their Houses on the Sabbath-day or evening after, or at any other time."[56] Finally in 1679, after the "Reforming Synod" at Boston had declared that "Most of the evils that abound amongst us, proceed from defects as to family government,"[57] the tithingmen were ordered to attend to disorders of every kind in the families under their charge.[58]

This legislation was directed against negligent heads of families. There was no occasion for conflict between the state and the gov-ernor of a well-ordered family, for the avowed purpose of both was the same: to enforce the laws of God. Sometimes the courts even dismissed lawbreakers to be dealt with by their family governors. When Increase Winn was presented at the Middlesex Court for contempt of authority, his master informed the court, "I doe not question but the instruccions and Correction he hath allready had, will hellp him to be more watchfull for time to come." The court considered the correction adequate even though it had been only "to convince him of his vilde carriag which he did acknowleg and bewaile with teares."[59] Similarly Joseph Perkins, presented at Essex Court for striking Josiah White, was discharged when the court was "informed that his father had given him correction for his fault";[60] and in the case of Elizabeth Hunt and Abigail Burn-

---

[55] *Massachusetts Laws of 1672*, p. 235.
[56] Ibid., p. 250.
[57] Cotton Mather, *Magnalia*, II, 323.
[58] *Massachusetts Laws of 1672*, p. 270.
[59] Middlesex Files, folder 24, group 2.
[60] *Essex Court Records*, VII, 193 (April 1679).

ham, two little girls who carried on a feud during church services, the court "judged them both culpable of disturbance and disorder in the meeting house, but being under family government, ordered their parents to correct them for offences past and to keep them in better order for the time to come."[61]

Husbands and wives, parents and children, masters and servants —these made the family that state and church must protect and preserve as the foundation of social order. But every family reached beyond these relationships in a network of kinship that also helped to sustain the bonds of society. Puritans felt the obligations of minor relationships only slightly less than those of their immediate families. Although the Great Migration to the New World had split many families from their English connections, they did their best to keep in touch by mail and to recognize the ties that bound them, even to the second or third generation. Samuel Sewall, for example, wrote letter after letter to relatives in England, recording the births, marriages, and deaths of his family and demanding from his correspondents similar accounts of his "dear relations" there. Sewall's dear relations were legion. In the course of his diary and letterbook he found occasion to speak of at least forty-eight cousins, and since thirty-eight of these bore different last names, it is probable, though he fails to mention it, that he was also acquainted with other members of their families.[62]

Sewall could claim such a multitude of relatives because he recognized kinship with persons far beyond the limits we would today hold within the family pale. Puritans addressed as brothers,

[61] Ibid., V, 306.

[62] The names of those to whom he refers are as follows (he frequently omitted the first name, simply calling them "cousin Brattle," "cousin Burges" etc.) : Allen, Andrews, Atwell, Baker, Gilbert Bear, Brattle, Burges, Carter, Nathaniel Dummer, Subael Dummer, Thomas Dummer, Fisk, Fissenden, John Fowle, Love Fowle, Mary Hate, Jane Holt, Thomas Holt, Edward Hull, Hunt, Lapworth, Joseph Moodey, Newman, Elizabeth Noyes, Pierce, Powers, Anna Quinsey, Daniel Quinsey, Edmund Quinsey, Rolf, Ephraim Savage, Mary Savage, William Savil, William Sellen, Henry Sewall, Jonathan Sewall, Margaret Sewall, Short, John Stork, Mercy Stork, Samuel Stork, Sarah Stork, Thomas Stork, Swett, John Tappin, Wells, and John Wendell.

sisters, parents, and cousins individuals with whom they were connected only by the more remote ties of marriage. For instance, after Fitz-John Winthrop's daughter married the son of Mrs. Robert Livingston, Winthrop wrote that lady assuring her of his love for her son, and advising her that "being related to you in a neerer than the neere relation of friendship I will take all opportunity to express my sence of it and that it will very much please me to be called Your most affectionate Brother, John Winthrop."[63] The Winthrop family admitted even remoter connections than this. After John Winthrop, Jr., had married the daughter of Edmund Reade and Hugh Peter had married Reade's widow, Winthrop addressed Peter as father, and John Winthrop, Sr., addressed him as brother.[64]

The death of a spouse and remarriage of the remaining partner further enlarged and complicated the web of relationships; for although a man might gain a whole new set of relations by a new marriage, he did not lose his first wife's relations by her death: he still addressed her kin as his own and still treated them with the same deference. After Edmund Pinson's first wife died, he married again without consulting her parents. When difficulties in this second match brought him to the Middlesex County Court, he laid his misfortunes to the fact that he had not shown more filial piety to his deceased wife's parents. He confessed to the court "that he is and was Guilty of Disobedience to his first wifes parients— who were Godly and Religious, In that he'did not make them Acquainted and take their Advice In his present match, but rather with Esau to the Greife of his parients chose more for affection, then for Religion and therefore may he feare this Evell is Com upon him. . . ."[65] Pinson obviously believed that his relationship to the family of his first wife endured beyond her death. Presumably his second wife felt herself included in that relationship,

[63] Massachusetts Historical Society *Collections*, sixth series, III, 68.
[64] Massachusetts Historical Society *Collections*, fourth series, VI, 91n; R. C. Winthrop, *The Life and Letters of John Winthrop*, II, 131.
[65] Middlesex Files, folder 42, group 3.

for the new wife of a widower became related not only to his natural family, but to all the kin of his first wife as well.[66] Margaret Tyndal, in marrying the elder John Winthrop, assumed an intimate relationship not only to his parents (see Adam Winthrop's letter to her, p. 60) but also to the families of his two former wives. In a letter to him written in June 1627 she said, "my brother Jenney remembers his love to you."[67] Her "brother Jenney" was, in our terms, the brother-in-law of her husband's previous wife! Since second and third marriages were common in the seventeenth century, a bewildering series of relationships was created between a large number of families.

The reason for extending the ties of relationship so far was not simply sentimental. Puritans believed that relations by marriage deserved equal recognition with those by birth, because they understood literally the Biblical dictum that man and wife are one flesh. They seldom used the term "in law," because the relationships to which we customarily apply that qualification existed for them in fact as well as in law: so closely were man and wife bound to each other and to each other's relatives, that marriage with a deceased wife's sister was supposed to involve incest. The ministers of Boston pronounced their judgment that

'Tis the law of our God, in Lev. xviii. 6, "none of you shall approach [in a marriage] unto any that is near of kin to him." Now, the kindred betwixt a man and his own wife's sister, is of the nearest sort: For, *Inter Virum et mulierem non contrahitur affinitas, sed ipsi sunt affinitas causa:* so then this affinity is not less than *in primo genere,* and therefore unlawful. It is likewise the concurrent sense of the greatest divines (particularly asserted in the Assemblies "confession of faith;") that of what degree any one is of consanguinity to his wife, in the same degree of affinity is that person to the husband. And that an husband is forbidden to marry with the *consanguines* of his wife, by the same rule that consanguines are forbidden to marry among themselves. And this assertion may be demonstrated from the *rules* given in the eight-

---

[66] The same course was true, *mutatis mutandis,* of the new husband of a widow.
[67] *Winthrop Papers,* I, 355.

eenth chapter of Leviticus. Wherefore, as a man may not marry his own sister, so not the sister of his wife, which is one flesh with him.[68]

Samuel Sewall, who felt repulsed by any marriage in which there was so much as a "smell of relation" between the parties,[69] wrote earnestly to his cousin John on February 23, 1703/4: "You tell me you have been advised to marry the Widow of your Cousin German. Tis a pity that any have been so Unadvisd themselvs, as to prompt you to do a needless thing, about which Advice is needed, to know whether it be Lawfull or No . . . it is by Casuists laid down as a Rule in these Cases, That Degrees of Consanguinity and Affinity do equally affect Marriage. . . . Now if the Scripture Reckons Grandfathers, Fathers: the Scripture likewise Reckons Cousins Germans among Brothers and Sisters, and so uncapable of Intermarriage."[70]

The substantial existence which a Puritan attributed to marital bonds accounts for the large number of kin to whom he acknowledged relation and also helps to explain his attitude toward them. Sewall told of love for his "deare relations," and Fitz-John Winthrop wished to be considered the "affectionate brother" of a lady whom he may never have seen. These declarations may have expressed real sentiments, but they were doubtless made with some consciousness of duty; for it was a Christian duty to love one's relatives. God had, of course, commanded his subjects to love all their fellow men and not just their relatives, but where it was impossible for a man to show an equal love to all, God required that he give his relatives first consideration. "We are more bound," William Ames explained, "to place our love on those whom God hath by some speciall neernesse or communion commended to us then on others." Though a Christian should exclude no one from his love, he should vary the amount expended on each person according to the intimacy of the connection. A man must love his wife more than anyone else in the world, because the bond between man

---

[68] Cotton Mather, *Magnalia*, II, 252.
[69] Sewall, "Diary," III, 398.
[70] Sewall, "Letter-Book," I, 291.

and wife was the closest in the world. He must love other relatives in proportion, "those that are neerest to be most loved," and all relatives, other things being equal, "more to be loved then strangers."[71] We have already noticed that when Fitz-John Winthrop objected to acquiring Mr. Newman as a relative, his father advised him that he must not alter his affection to his sister if she did marry Newman; the father also insisted that Fitz-John should have an "indeared affection" toward Mr. Newman as well, "if the Lord shall please to put him in that relation to us."[72]

The easiest way of showing love for relatives was to display interest and concern for them by keeping up acquaintances with as many as possible whether they lived nearby or far away. A more concrete way was to favor them in business dealings. Since a Puritan merchant usually had kin in England, he could practice the duty of love by conducting his business in the mother country through them. This procedure, of course, had advantages for him as well as for his relatives: since they presumably felt the same affection for him that he felt for them, he could trust them to dispose of his cargoes advantageously. Thus the bonds of commerce became in many cases synonymous with bonds of kin. This phenomenon can be observed very clearly in the letterbook of Samuel Sewall's father-in-law, John Hull, the foremost merchant of the Bay Colony in his time.[73] Hull's correspondence from Boston with "Uncle Parris" and with "Cousins Daniel Allin and Thomas Buckham" in England reveals a very sore trial of the family bonds, but in spite of temptation and vexation family loyalty kept the goods flowing in the proper channels.

At the beginning of the letterbook, about 1670, the correspondence shows that Hull had on hand a tremendous supply of hats, sent to him by Uncle Parris to be sold on a joint account. Hull wrote that he would be glad to sell anything that his uncle sent on a separate account, but that he would not sell anything (especially

[71] William Ames, *The Marrow of Sacred Divinity*, p. 302.
[72] Massachusetts Historical Society *Collections*, fifth series, VIII, 48.
[73] John Hull, manuscript Letter-Book in the library of the American Antiquarian Society at Worcester, Massachusetts.

not these hats) on their joint account, unless he, Hull, should expressly ask that it be shipped. Soon after this letter Uncle Parris died. Hull's cousins Daniel Allin and Thomas Buckham undertook to settle the estate and carry on the business. Their first action was to request payment for the hats. When Hull refused, they sent a series of abusive letters upbraiding him for not paying his debts and for sending poor or overpriced shipments of various goods to them. Hull replied that he did not take the hats on joint account and so felt no responsibility for them. He would do with them whatever they pleased, either return them to England or sell them for what he could get and send the proceeds. To the charge that he invested their money unwisely in the goods which he had shipped, he apologized by urging them to do business somewhere else: "And so likewise deare Cozen If you thinke I doe not Invest youre monyes so well as some others might do I will most freely render what by youre next I shall have received in mony to any person to whom you shall give your order, and I say not this in any heate or displeasure of mind, but out of a sober sence of my Less Capacity then some others becaus of my habitacion it having been alwayes out of the croud of trade where is the best opertunyty of buying and selling."[74]

This offer called the bluff of the English cousins so far as concerned Hull's business capacities. They continued to do business with him. But they also continued to plague him about the hats. When he sent some money to pay personal debts, they applied it to the partial payment of Uncle Parris's hats, and Buckham spread the story in London that Hull was "a very knave and deserve to bee soe posted upon the Exchange."[75] Hull indignantly but with great restraint reprimanded Buckham with a series of letters, in which he addressed him as "Angry Cozen" or "Unkind Cozen," and advised him that

iff in an[y] of my Actions you may thinke ther is any ground of Suspition, Coz the Love and duty of a kins man should have

---

[74] Ibid., August 23, 1672.
[75] Ibid., January 13, 1672/3.

obliged you to have writt to mee about it and have taken my
answer and iff there had bene any error not to have disclosed it
unless I had persisted in denieing of all Reasonable satisfaction. . . .
I have Ever tooke you as my Loveing Coz and I de[sire] to take
you soe still and therfore asoone as I heare of this I doe thus
plai[nly] tell you of it and therfore desire you to do so by me iff I
dought any one of my friends Love I will tell them off it and not
other men and I pra[y] you do so by me else I shall desire I may
have no more to doe w[ith] you in this world for the sin of Back-
biteing and slandering is to be h[ated] by all good men I desire
therfore I may heare from you fully by Let[ter] Ueither make out
my faults that I may bee Ashamed of them and give you satisfaction or Confess your owne faults and give me satisfaction and
indeed Coz Such is my Love and affection to you all that I can
readyly overlooke many injuryes and bee willing to do you good
with my whole hearte according to my Capacity. . . .[76]

Hull's anger turned his apologies for his own deficiencies in business investment to complaints against his cousins. He accused them
of sending cloth full of holes; and when they complained of the
high price of a load of logwood, he lectured them for not leaving him
more liberty to buy advantageously: their demand for an immediate shipment necessitated his buying when the market was high
and deprived him of funds to make other advantageous purchases.
He continued adamant about the hat question, for when he un-
crated the hats, he found that they were all too large for New
England heads and furthermore had been reduced to shreds by the
moths. By April 29, 1676, he was even suggesting, with great pro-
tests of affection, that he might himself be forced to do business
elsewhere.

Mr. Tho. Buckam, by mr. wells in mr. ox ship And unkind Cousin
. . . I am unwilling to be so unkind as to goe from you (Cousin)
to any other (though I have many Invitations) unless you should
by a constant course of unkindness utterly discourage me. Yet even
then I hope I shall not cease to pray for you and all my dear
Cousins, that (though I should have ill will requited me for my

[76] Ibid., January 13, 1672/3.

good) you and yours may be saved. I thank God I have a *Kinsmans* heart to you; though you have not had a faithfull and friendly Kinsman's *tongue* toward me And shall be willing truely to doe and endeavour your good, though you should continue to requite me evil: But I hope the Lord will enlighten you to see that I never did you, nor any of my friends any wrong. And I hope I never shall. I am sure I have lost some hundreds of pounds because I was loath to grieve my dear unkle. For had I sent back from time to time the unvendible goods, sent me time after time against my express orders, or had I refused to accept the care and charge to sell and dispose that three thousand and seven hundred pounds of My unckles, when I was last in England, I had freed my self from damage and loss, and you could not have had any pretence, or colour to have spoken hardly of me. But I am not pleased to harp upon this unpleasant string. I much rather chuse in loving and utter oblivion to bury all unkindnesses, and desire I may, and hope I shall walk in the fear of the Lord, who is the searcher of all hearts, and before whom are both all my wayes, and all other mens.

And Cousin I present you once again with my dear & loving Respects to my Cousin Mary your loving wife, and to all your children: and shall endeavour to walk towards you all as a real Kinsman, as one that truely loved honoured and respected your loving father, and forgets all matters past, as if they had never been: Provided they be not reiterated and renewed by your selvs: And in hope thereof shall in my writings and actions shew (through that grace of the Lord) that I doe mean as I speak. And therefore at present I salute you all in the Lord . . . your truly loving Cousin J.H.[77]

Hull's business was, of course, not limited to relatives, but he undeniably favored them and put up with treatment he would never have stood from a stranger.

The relatives across the ocean were not the only ones favored: wherever possible, Puritans also helped their New England kin in business dealings. As Hull grew old, he passed much of his trade along to his son-in-law. On December 27, 1680, he wrote to Cousin

---

[77] Ibid., April 29, 1676.

Allen about another and more successful shipment of hats: "I received your glasses and hats, and have obtained my son-in-law, Samuel Sewall, to take your consignment of them. He hath sold your hats and some glasses; and as he can sell the rest, and receive in, so he will render you an account, and make you return; and I hope with prudence and faithfulness, for he is both prudent and faithful."[78] Sewall did most of his business not with Allen, but with another cousin of Hull's, Edward Hull. Shortly after his marriage Sewall opened relations with Edward by the following letter:

MR. EDWARD H. AND LOVING COUSIN, Although I never saw you, yet your Name, Affinity to me, and what I have heard concerning you, make me desirous of your acquaintance and Correspondence. Your Remembrance to me in my Father's I take very kindly. And I, with your Cousin, my Wife, do by these, heartily re-salute you. . . . Sir, My Father in Law hath consigned to yourself two hh of Peltry, to be for his and my joint Account, as you will see by the Letter and Invoice. I shall not need to en-treat your utmost care for the best Disposal of them according to what is prescribed you: which shall oblige the writer of these Lines, your loving friend and Kinsman.[79]

By 1683 Sewall was recommending that Edward send some busi-ness to brother Stephen at Salem: "Cousin My Brother Stephen Sewall hath conveniency for Shopkeepng. If you or any other shall at his order and desire Credit him I believe he will industriously endeavour payment: And hath a House and Land at Salem, and some other considerable Estate."[80] When his daughter Betty mar-ried Grove Hirst, Sewall wrote to his friend Nathaniel Higginson in London:

Sir, I writt you a large Letter this morning in my own Concern. This is to pray your Favour for my Son-in-Law Mr. Grove Hirst; that if you make any Consignment of Merchandize, that may not

---

[78] "The Diaries of John Hull," *Archaeologia Americana* (transactions and collections of the American Antiquarian Society), III, 124.

[79] Sewall, "Diary," I, 25.

[80] John Hull, Letterbook, December 5, 1683, marginal notes.

be so convenient for your own Relations considering the place of their Dwelling, you would send them to him, who dwells in Town, and is a very industrious and Skillfull Merchant, and a faithfull man. If you please so far to take notice of him, you will still further oblige your already very much obliged friend. And if you be a member of the Corporation, that you would favour him with a Bill of Exchange on Mr. Francis Clark, who is partner with him, and is now going home in this Fleet, if he desire it. I am Sir, your most humble Servt.[81]

When Grove Hirst died in 1717, Sewall tried to save as much of his business as possible for another relative. On the very day of Hirst's death Sewall wrote to cousin Samuel Storke of London:

I suppose you are not unacquainted with Mr. Samuell Sewall Son of Major Sewall of Salem. He is an accomplish'd Merchant and dwells in Town. If you might transfer the business wherein you Employ'd Mr. Hirst, upon him, I hope it would be for your Profit; and you would therein very much gratify me. His Brother Jonathan Sewall liv'd with Mr. Hirst several years, who was pleased with his Skillfull and faithfull Services and has often in my hearing given him a very good Character. Jonathan now dwells with his Brother and joyns with him in his Ship-Chandlers Business.[82]

The next day he wrote to Cousin John Storke,

I am Thankfull to you and others that may be Concerned for the profitable businesse You Imployed Mr. Hirst in. And now if you Should See meet to Transfer your Buisnesse to my Cousin Mr. Samuel Sewall Eldest Son of my Brother Major Sewall of Salem, It would Very much gratifie me. He has a good Storehouse Just by Mr. Hirst's and I hope would Transact for you with Integrity, ability and application. His Brother Jonathan Sewall dwells with him, who formerly lived Several Years with Mr. Hirst who gave him a Very good character; and he understands and is well acquainted with Mr. Hirst's affairs.[83]

[81] Sewall, "Letter-Book," I, 336.
[82] Ibid., II, 75.
[83] Ibid., II, 76.

The final episode in this chronicle is a letter to Samuel Storke on October 2, 1728. By this time Grove Hirst's children had grown up, and one of them, Hannah, had married another merchant, Nathaniel Balston. When Balston undertook a trip to London, Sewall provided him with a letter of recommendation to cousin Storke: "I send these by Mr. Nathaniel Balston Merchant, who lately married my dear Grandchild Mrs. Hannah Hirst. I intreat your Favour for him, and Assistance of him in what he may stand in need; in doing which you will much oblige me; I shall take it as done to my self."[84]

Thus in their economic, as in their ecclesiastical and political affairs, the Puritans assigned a major role to their families. As long as families were well ordered, as long as men respected the logic of relationships, corruption would be restrained within bounds, and society would escape those gross iniquities that invited divine judgment. So at least the Puritans believed and accordingly took every precaution to order their families as God demanded. But the weaknesses of fallen man proved more insidious than they had suspected, and in the very act of devoting themselves to their families, they upset the order of creation they meant to preserve and threatened the goal to which church, state, and family alike were dedicated.

[84] Ibid., II, 254.

VII

Puritan Tribalism

*T*HE preceding chapters have dealt with the effect of Puritanism on the family. It is impossible to measure the extent of the effect, but I have tried to show how a set of religious ideas influenced the way members of a family regarded one another. One may now fairly inquire whether the family did not in turn affect Puritanism, whether the natural relationships between husband and wife and between parents and children did not influence the way Puritans thought about God and the church.

The Puritans themselves would certainly have been reluctant to admit an influence in this direction. Though man delights to create God in his own image, the Puritans strove hard to avoid doing so and whitewashed churches and smashed idols wherever they recognized them. But even the Puritans were unable to escape entirely from the temptation to think of God in human forms. They could remove from their churches the figures of Christ and his angels, but they were defenseless against figures of speech. In sermon after sermon the ministers of New England explained to their congregations that the true believer was wedded to his God in a holy marriage. "It is a marriage-covenant that we make with God," said Peter Bulkeley; and, he reasoned, "therefore we must doe as the Spouse doth, resigne up our selves to be ruled and governed according to his will."[1]

The idea that God was actually married to his saints was very

---

[1] Bulkeley, *Gospel-Covenant*, p. 50.

comforting, for a marriage was not easily dissolved. The believer
might commit many petty sins without being cast off by God.
"Weaknesses do not debar us from mercy," said Thomas Shepard;
"nay, they incline God the more. The husband is bound to bear
with the wife, as being the weaker vessel; and shall we think God
will exempt himself from his own rule, and not bear with his weak
spouse?"[2] Bulkeley put the case just as appealingly when he said
that with the Christian and his God it was "as it is betweene man
and wife, though shee be foolish, passionate, and wilfull; yet these
doe not breake the Covenant of marriage, so long as shee remaineth
faithfull."[3]

Of course the ministers used other metaphors to describe the relations of God and man. The analogies of king and subject, master
and servant, soul and body were frequently employed. But marriage, which the Puritans regarded as the highest relationship between mortals, was generally accepted as the closest comparison to
the believer's union with God.[4] So much did the metaphor become
a part of the accepted theological vocabulary that Samuel Sewall,
during a visit to England, was disappointed when an English
minister failed to use it: "March 10, 1688/9 would have heard mr.
Goldwire, but mr. Beamont the Minister of Fareham preached from
Ps. 45, 15. Doct. Interest and Duty of Christians to rejoice in Christ
made good profitable Sermons; but I think might have been more
so, if had us'd the Metaphor of Bridegroom and Bride, which
heard not of.[5]

The comparison could be extended to explain many of the central
doctrines of Christian theology. Did the minister wish to expound
the theory of the redemption? His sermon became clear to his listeners if he showed them that redemption was a result of marriage to

[2] Thomas Shepard, *Works*, I, 50.
[3] Bulkeley, *Gospel-Covenant*, p. 103.
[4] See Shepard, *Works*, II, 31: "The soul hence gives itself, like one espoused
to her husband, to the Lord Jesus. . . . Servants give work for their wages, and
masters give wages for their work, but husbands and wives give themselves one
unto another. . . ."
[5] Sewall, "Diary," I, 299.

Christ. Thomas Hooker disposed of innumerable theological complications when he said:

As when the wife is betrothed and married to a man, all her old debts are laid upon her husband, and the law meddles no more with her: and secondly, all his lands, at least the third part of them are made over to her. What shee hath in point of debt is put over to him: so all our sinnes and debts of corruptions are laid upon Christ, and all the rich fefments of grace and mercy in Christ, are made over to a beleever, and hence a beleever comes to be acquitted and justified before God.[6]

The distinction between betrothal and marriage served a useful purpose in differentiating between the imperfect holiness attainable in this world and the complete sanctification of the next. John Cotton argued that the Day of Judgment "shall be our Marriage day." "Now," he explained, "we are but betrothed to Christ, we are now so coy that Christ hath much adoe to get our good will. . . . For we are now full of whorish and adulterous lusts, wherefore the Apostle exhorts the *Corinthians,* and in them all us, to cleanse our selves from all filthinesse of flesh and spirit."[7] In this application of the metaphor it became the function of the ministers to serve as the "friends" of the bridegroom, that is, according to the custom of the time, to arrange the match. Cotton told his congregation, "It's the work of the Ministers of the Gospel, to drive a match between you and Christ." Samuel Arnold, in addressing his fellow ministers

[6] Thomas Hooker, *The Soules Exaltation* (London, 1638), p. 133. Cf. Increase Mather, *Practical Truths Plainly Delivered* (Boston, 1718), p. 60: "There can be no Law-suits against them [believers] *Uxori lis non intenditur.* The Husband is responsible for his Wives debts."

[7] John Cotton, *Practical Commentary upon John*, p. 227. Cf. Increase Mather, *Practical Truths Plainly Delivered*, p. 54: "In this Life Believers are Espoused to Christ. At his Second coming will be the Consummation of the Marriage. Christ will then come as a Bridegroom." Cf. Jonathan Mitchell, *A Discourse of the Glory to Which God hath Called Believers by Jesus Christ* (London, 1677), p. 30: ". . . our present state is but an Espousal, the consummation of the Marriage is at the day of Judgment; thence follows the full enjoyment each of other in Heaven, when Christ hath carried his Spouse home to his Fathers house. . . ."

of Massachusetts, told them that "Christ is the Bridegroom, we are or ought to be the Bridegrooms Friends."[8]

Somewhat inconsistently, but in keeping with the general comparison, Cotton in another work compared the public worship of God in church to the bodily love of husband and wife. In *A Brief Exposition with Practical Observations upon the Whole Book of Canticles,* he wrote:

[*For delights, or in delights*] It is an allusion to the marriage-bed, which is the delights of the Bridegroom, and Bride. This marriage-bed is the publick worship of God in the Congregation of the Church as *Cant.* 3.1.

The publick Worship of God is the bed of loves: where, 1. Christ embraceth the souls of his people, and casteth into their hearts the immortal seed of his Word, and Spirit, *Gal.* 4.19. 2. The Church conceiveth and bringeth forth fruits to Christ.[9]

In like fashion idolatry was called adultery, the Roman Church a whore, and the casting off of backsliders a divorce.[10]

As human marriage implied a family with parents and children, the simile could be extended to make all Christians a family with God as the father. In this aspect of the comparison it was emphasized that Christ was the bridegroom, who introduced the believer into the family of God. Thus a part of the Trinity became more easy to understand. In some respects God was a father, in others a

[8] John Cotton, *Practical Commentary upon John*, p. 320; Samuel Arnold, *David Serving his Generation* (Cambridge, 1674), p. 11.

[9] (London, 1655), p. 209. Cf. John Cotton, *Christ the Fountaine of Life*, pp. 36–37: "And looke what affection is between Husband and Wife, hath there been the like affection in your soules towards the Lord Jesus Christ? Have you a strong and hearty desire to meet him in the bed of loves, when ever you come to the Congregation, and desire you to have the seeds of his grace shed abroad in your hearts, and bring forth the fruits of grace to him, and desire that you may be for him, and for none other? . . ."

[10] For examples see Samuel Mather, *A Testimony from the Scripture against Idolatry and Superstition* (Cambridge, 1670), p. 14; Cotton, *Practical Commentary upon John*, p. 101, *Christ the Fountaine of Life*, p. 190; Richard Mather, *Church Government and Church-Covenant Discussed* (London, 1643), p. 9, *An Apologie of the Churches in New-England for Church-Covenant*, p. 40.

husband. When Christ married a believer, God adopted that believer as a child, so that Samuel Willard could entitle a book about the benefits of divine grace *The Child's Portion*.[11] In that book Willard explained that our "sonship" was the result of "our Marriage to Christ; so that by becoming his Spouse . . . we are made the Children of God." [12] Similarly, John Cotton wrote that *"Adoption* is properly the work of the Father, but Christ being the naturall Son of God, we must be knit unto him, before we can be accounted Sons."[13]

The advantages of being a bride of Christ and a child of God were frequently explained. Willard itemized the benefits as follows:

1. He [God] will certainly provide for them . . . if others in a Family suffer want, yet the Children shall certainly be taken care for, as long as there is anything to be had: they are hard times indeed when Children are denied that which is needful for them. . . .
2. He will protect them from all harms and injuries. . . .
3. He will uphold them from falling: he will take them by their hand, and stay their steps for them, sustein them, keep them from undoing themselves. . . .
4. He will counsel and direct them. . . .
5. He will assist and strengthen them. . . .
6. He will Correct and Chasten them for their Faults. . . .
7. He will commend and encourage them when they do well. . . .[14]

It may be that this conception of theology in domestic terms was simply a convenient literary and rhetorical device or a mere repetition of the predominant imagery of the Bible. But in the preceding passage Willard seems to have taken the analogy almost literally, as though the believer were actually a spouse of Christ and a child of God. This passage is not an isolated example. Other ministers based arguments upon the comparison in the same way. Increase Mather argued that "since Believers are Married to Christ, Christ and all that belongs to him is theirs. They have an Interest in his Person:

[11] Boston, 1684.
[12] P. 11.
[13] John Cotton, *The Covenant of Grace*, p. 191.
[14] Willard, *The Childs Portion*, p. 15.

They are his and He theirs."[15] Thomas Hooker reasoned: "The Husband and Wife in comliness, should co-habit in the same place, and dwel together. . . . Christ the Husband is gone into his own, out of a far Countrey; and therefore he cannot but affectionately desire the coming of his Bride unto him."[16] And John Norton urged the necessity of union with Christ by stating, "As a Spouse is first married to the person, *i.e.* her Husband, before she enjoyeth any conjugal communion with him: so, we first by faith receive the Person of Christ, before we are made partakers of the benefits of Christ, bestowed upon Beleevers."[17]

The metaphor seems to have dominated Puritan thought so completely as to suggest that the Puritans' religious experiences in some way duplicated their domestic experiences. This is not to imply that the Christianity of the Puritans was merely a sublimation of filial or sexual impulses, but certainly there was a large element of sublimation in it. The Puritans even thought of human affection for a wife or a husband or a parent as a rival to the affection for God. Husbands and wives were often directed by ministers to save their greatest love, not for each other, but for God,[18] while single persons were advised to substitute love of God for forbidden lusts of the flesh. "Art thou troubled with lust after Women?" John Cotton asked; "and God calls thee not to Marriage, why turn the strength of thy affection to another Spouse, *that is white and ruddy, the fairest of ten thousand.* The more you set your heart to consider, how amiable, and beautiful, and excellent he is, you shall finde he will so satisfie your heart, that you will finde little content in any other thing besides."[19]

---

[15] Increase Mather, *Practical Truths Plainly Delivered*, p. 59.

[16] Thomas Hooker, *A Comment upon Christ's Last Prayer*, p. 357.

[17] John Norton, *The Orthodox Evangelist* (London, 1654), p. 194.

[18] See chapter II above.

[19] John Cotton, *A Practical Commentary upon John*, p. 131. Cf. Thomas Hooker, *A Comment upon Christ's Last Prayer*, p. 178: "Let not the Lord have the leanest of our Love, the Female Affection, the leavings of any thing here below: We had the chief of his Love, let us lay out the choycest of our Affections wholly and only upon himself before al Creatures we prize." Cf. Letters of Henry Dorney copied by Ebenezer Pemberton, manuscript in the library of the Massachusetts Historical Society: "Indeed, I scarce know a greater sign of

One may find further evidence of sublimation in John Winthrop's "Christian Experience," written during the interval between the death of his second wife and his marriage to a third:

Lookinge over some lettres of kindnesse that had passed between my first wife and me, and beinge thereby affected with the remembrance of that entire and sweet love that had been sometymes between us, God brought me by that occasion in to suche a heavenly meditation of the love betweene Christ and me, as ravished my heart with unspeakable ioye; methought my soule had as familiar and sensible society with him as my wife could have with the kindest husbande; I desired no other happinesse but to be embraced of him; I held nothinge so deere that I was not willinge to parte with for him; I forgatt to looke after my supper, and some vaine things that my heart lingered after before; then came such a calme of comforte over my heart, as revived my spirits, sett my minde and conscience at sweet liberty and peace. . . .

This comfort that I had in his sweet love drewe me to deale with him as I was wont to doe with my earthly welbeloved, who beinge ever in the eye of my affection, I greedily imployed everye opportunitye to be a messinger of the manifestation of my love, by lettres, &c: so did I now with my deare lord Christ; I delighted to meditate of him, to praye to him, and to the Father in him (for all was one with me), to remember his sweet promises, etc: for I was well assured that he tooke all that I did in good parte.[20]

The meditation continues at some length in the same vein. Together with Cotton's statement, it suggests that in some instances at least religious sentiments might be simply a substitute for the love of a husband or wife. Some lines of Anne Bradstreet, written during an absence of her husband, have the same implication:

> Tho: husband dear bee from me gone
> Whom I doe love so well;

Christ's conjugal love, than by his providence to render all other things and conditions here to be unlovely and undesirable: for then the affections have no where else to centre but in Christ; and that makes them go out strong that way."

[20] Winthrop, *Life and Letters of John Winthrop,* I, 105–107.

I have a more beloved one
Whose comforts far excell.[21]

Thus while the Puritans sought to create a society in which everyone should obey the laws of God, they came to think of God himself not as an inscrutable and almighty Being but as a husband or father, or in the words of Increase Mather, as the "Wisest and Richest bridegroom."[22]

In creating churches and preaching the word in them Puritans went even further toward domesticating the Almighty than they did in theology. Here the influence of family relations on their thinking was more direct, for in their churches God tended to become not merely a husband or father but the husband or father only of families that belonged to orthodox New England churches. Puritans of course thought of their God as the one God of the universe; but they made him so much their own, in the guise of making themselves his, that eventually and at times he took on the character of a tribal deity.

The impetus toward this transformation came from the natural fondness of parents for their children combined with the duty they felt to nurture children in God's ways. The Puritans had come to New England for a variety of reasons, but one of the strongest, by their own account, was the urge to perpetuate pure religion among their children. By the latter half of the seventeenth century it had become an accepted tradition that the founders of New England had left the old world for the sake of their children. Samuel Willard told the New Englanders of 1682 that "the main errand which brought your Fathers into this Wilderness, was not only that they might themselves enjoy, but that they might settle for their Children, and leave them in full possession of the free, pure, and uncorrupted libertyes of the Covenant of Grace."[23] Increase Mather, addressing the younger generation in 1679, reminded them that "it was for your sakes especially, that your Fathers ventured their

[21] Anne Bradstreet, *Works*, p. 35.
[22] Increase Mather, *Practical Truths Plainly Delivered*, p. 59.
[23] Samuel Willard, *Covenant-Keeping the Way to Blessedness*, p. 117.

lives upon the rude waves of the vast Ocean."[24] At the same time John Wilson reminded the older generation that "you came hither for your Children, Sons and Daughters, and for your Grand-children to be under the Ordinances of God."[25]

The ministers emphasized this tradition for a particular purpose: it made the younger generation conscious of their responsibility to maintain the true religion, and it reminded the older generation of the importance of keeping their children in line.[26] It was, however, more than a convenient myth created for that purpose. Thomas Shepard recalled in his autobiography that at the time of his removal from England he "considered how sad a thing it would be for me to leave my wife and child, (if I should dy) in that rude place of the North [*i.e.* Yorkshire] where was nothing but barbarous wickednes generally and how sweet it would be to leave them among gods people tho poore."[27] In spite of its Indians, the wilderness was to Shepard the place of God's people, while England was a place of barbarous wickedness. Other founders felt the same way. One of them, writing anonymously of the reasons which justified the exodus to New England, stated that Puritan children were too much exposed to evil in English schools and colleges. "The Fountaines of Learning and Religion," he said,

are soe corrupted as (besides the unsupportable charge of there education) most children (even the best witts and of fairest hopes)

---

[24] Increase Mather, *A Call from Heaven*, p. 42.

[25] John Wilson, *A Seasonable Watchword* (Cambridge, 1677), p. 8.

[26] Willard, for example, after making the statement quoted above, told his congregation that "it was their love to your Souls that embarked them in this designe, and it will be horrible ingratitude in you to slight it . . . and [you] will be unworthy heirs of your Father's Estates, if you do not prosecute their begun designs" (*Covenant-Keeping the Way to Blessedness*, p. 118). Eleazer Mather spoke to the older generation to the same effect: "I pray consider, what was the thing proposed? *why came you into this land? was it not mainly with respect to the rising Generation?* And what with respect to them? was it to leave them a rich and wealthy people? was it to leave them Houses, Lands, Livings? Oh no: but to leave God in the midst of them" (*Serious Exhortation*, p. 16).

[27] Colonial Society of Massachusetts *Publications*, XXVII, 375–376.

are perverted, corrupted, and utterlie overthrowne by the multitude of evill examples and the licentious government of those seminaries, where men straine at knatts and swallowe camells, use all severity for mainetaynance of cappes and other accomplyments, but suffer all ruffianlike fashions and disorder in manners to passe uncontrolled.[28]

The Pilgrims found Holland no better than England. Bradford wrote concerning their troubles there that

of all sorowes most heavie to be borne, was that many of their children, by these occasions, and the great licentiousnes of youth in that countrie, and the manifold temptations of the place, were drawne away by evill examples into extravagante and dangerous courses, getting the raines off their necks, and departing from their parents. Some became souldiers, others tooke upon them farr viages by sea; and others some worse courses, tending to dissolutnes, and the danger of their soules, to the great greefe of their parents and dishonour of God. So that they saw their posteritie would be in danger to degenerate and be corrupted.[29]

In coming to the wilderness, then, the founders of New England hoped to protect their children from profanity. In the new world they expected to have the company of godly men like themselves. They miscalculated. To be sure, they could not have supposed that all the inhabitants of their new Canaan would be saints; they must have expected many scoundrels to show up—and they were prepared to deal with scoundrels—but they did not imagine that the emigration would bring to the shores of Massachusetts Bay such a horde of average, lusty Elizabethan Englishmen. The settlement had scarcely got under way before John Humfrey was advising Winthrop to look for another place of refuge and "to remove our choice people thither and to leave the mixt multitude (that will ever bee as thornes and prickes unto us) behind us."[30] Five years later Nathaniel Ward wrote to John Winthrop, Jr., that

---

[28] Winthrop, *Life and Letters of John Winthrop*, I, 310.
[29] William Bradford, *History of Plymouth Plantation*, I, 55.
[30] Massachusetts Historical Society *Collections*, fourth series, VI, 8 (December 12, 1630).

our thoughts and feares growe very sadd to see such multitudes of idle and profane young men, servants and others, with whome we must leave our children, for whose sake and safty we came over . . . we knowe this might have bene easily prevented by due and tymely care of such as had the opportunity in their hand; and if it be not yet remedied, we and many others must not only say, with greif, we have made an ill change, even from the snare to the pitt, but must meditate some safer refuge, if God will afford it. . . .[31]

No safer refuge was found. The number of unregenerate who crossed the ocean along with the saints was too great to banish from the land. It has been estimated that they amounted to four-fifths of the total population, and while this figure has rightly been challenged, it is quite possible that the godly were in a minority.[32] Ward had exaggerated, however, when he said that the removal to New England was a change from the snare to the pit. Here the godly at least controlled the government, as they definitely did not in old England. If they had not escaped from the company of the unregenerate, they had at least gained political power over them. No sin would be condoned, much less encouraged.

The Puritans nevertheless had to admit that their refuge in America was harboring a lot of unwanted guests. Their children were still exposed to the influence of evil men. Though the civil government could give visible proof, in stocks, jails, and whipping

[31] Ibid., VII, 24–25.

[32] The estimate of four-fifths, made by John G. Palfrey for the year 1670 by comparing the number of freemen with the estimated total of adult males, has been challenged by Samuel E. Morison on the ground that (a) not all church-members took advantage of their right to become freemen, and (b) in Roxbury in 1640, fifty-eight of sixty-nine householders (i.e., heads of households) were churchmembers. Morison admits that Palfrey's estimate may have been correct for 1670, but claims that the reason was the declension of the second generation, not the proportion of saints and sinners in the original migration. Morison would probably agree, however, that even in 1640 a majority of the total population were unregenerate by Puritan standards. Another authority, Perry Miller, accepts the figure of four-fifths as applying to the original migration. (See John G. Palfrey, *History of New England* (Boston, 1858–1890), III, 41n; Samuel E. Morison, *Builders of the Bay Colony* (Boston, 1930), pp. 339–346; Perry Miller and Thomas H. Johnson, eds., *The Puritans* (New York, 1938), p. 191.

posts, that sin did not pay in Massachusetts, yet children would inevitably gravitate toward the fascinating company of notorious sinners. "As Man's Nature enclines him to be Sociable," Samuel Willard ruminated, "so the Connate Corruption in fallen Man, disposeth him to evil Society; and Children early discover the Naughtiness of their hearts in this regard, by associating themselves, with such as are lewd. . . ."[33] Since so many of the lewd had found their way to the promised land, it was imperative that the children of the saints be urgently warned against mingling with them. "Let a man beware of his company," said Richard Mather. "He that delights to walk and talk with them that have the plague, it is no marvell if he catch infection."[34] Cotton Mather echoed his grandfather's words. In *The Young Mans Preservative* he explained that "there is a *Civility* to be expressed in your Carriage towards all men: But when it comes to the point of INTIMACY . . . there you will do well to use more of Reservation. . . . Briefly, all that you see, that are likely to Tempt you into any *Sin,* or to Poison your *Souls* with any Malignity; My *Young Men,* have as little to do with them as ever you can."[35] When the ministers instructed parents about the government of children, they always emphasized the importance of keeping them away from wicked companions. "Under this head of *Government,*" wrote Benjamin Wadsworth,

I might further say, you should restrain your Children *from bad company,* as far as possibly you can . . . *A companion of fools shall be destroyed.* If you would not have your Sons and Daughters destroyed, then keep them from ill company as much as may be. . . . You should not suffer your Children, needlessly to frequent *Taverns,* nor to be abroad *unseasonably on nights;* lest they're drawn into numberless hazards and mischiefs thereby: you can't be too careful in these matters.[36]

[33] Willard, *Compleat Body of Divinity,* p. 604.
[34] Richard Mather, *The Summe of Certain Sermons* (Cambridge, 1652), preface.
[35] Cotton Mather, *The Young Mans Preservative* (Boston, 1701), p. 43.
[36] Wadsworth, *Well-Ordered Family,* pp. 57–58.

Cotton Mather's advice was more vigorous. *"Charge* them," he told parents, "to avoid the snares of *Evil Company;* Terrify them with Warnings of those Deadly Snares. Often Repeat this *Charge* unto them, That if there be any *Vicious Company,* they shun them, as they would the *Plague* or the *Devil*."[37]

Countless examples of this kind of advice might be produced. They indicate a defensive, tribal attitude, growing at the heart of New England Puritanism. The ablest of the founders of New England, their eyes on larger horizons, were undismayed by the fact that man in America had proved to be, after all, man, still succumbing to temptation, still perishing, still tainted with original sin. In the first generation men like John Winthrop and Thomas Hooker held in check the tribal spirit in Puritanism and strove to make New England a beacon to the world, not a refuge from it. But later generations, losing sight of the errand on which the founders had come, succumbed more and more to tribalism. They preached and coaxed and prayed in order to save their children for Christ, but this very love for their children paralyzed the evangelical impulse that gave their religion meaning. They translated "Love thy neighbor" as "Love thy family."

Of course they did not entirely neglect the sinners who lived around them: they scrupulously punished every breach of the laws of God committed within their jurisdiction. But no visible reformation followed. Nor could they have expected one. They would have been the first to acknowledge that sin could not be extinguished by punishment alone, for they knew that only the Holy Spirit could destroy man's love for sinful ways. The punishment of sin in New England was aimed not so much at improving the sinners as it was at demonstrating to God that the rulers did not condone sin.[38] If the Puritans had really wished to free sinners from the bondage of corruption, they would have bent their greatest efforts at conversion.

They did, it is true, make some effort to convert the unregenerate

---

[37] Cotton Mather, *A Family Well-Ordered,* pp. 28–29.
[38] See Edmund S. Morgan, "The Case Against Anne Hutchinson," *New England Quarterly,* X, 635–649.

by compelling sinners and saints alike to attend church. Yet in organizing their churches they gave attention only to the saints. Anyone proposing to join a Puritan church had to prove to the satisfaction of the members that he was no longer in need of conversion. Though everyone had to attend, membership was confined to those who had already been converted. This exclusion of the unregenerate from membership may have been caused by an intransigent desire to cleanse the temple. The intransigence, however, stopped short of excluding the children of the saints even though a child could obviously not fulfill the requirement just stated.[39] While adults could enter the church only by proving their conversion, children automatically became members when their parents joined, and though unconverted they could remain members until they grew up. Then, in order to retain their membership, they too must experience conversion, but in the meantime they received all the privileges of membership except communion. The church was thus turned into an exclusive society for the saints and their children. Instead of an agency for bringing Christ to fallen man it became the means of perpetuating the gospel among a hereditary religious aristocracy. For the children of saints received not only the privilege of being admitted to membership without having been converted, but they also received the special attention of the ministry, directed at bringing about their conversion and insuring their continued membership.

When a New England minister preached the gospel, he did not ordinarily address himself to the masses who attended church by command of the state: he spoke either to the church members, who already had grace, or else to their children. When the Puritans were accused of neglecting the work of conversion, they denied the charge not on the ground that they converted ordinary sinners but on the ground that they converted their children. Thomas Welde in

[39] Not, at least, at the time when children were usually baptized, before they were a year old. The Puritans acknowledged the conversion of children as young as eight years old, but they never pretended that an infant in arms could enjoy the experience. (See Cotton Mather, *A Token for the Children of New England* (Boston, 1700).

An Answer to W. R. summarized the accusation and gave the answer. According to Welde, W. R. had claimed

That the end of our Ministry is onely the building up of men already converted, (as supposing our members are all reall saints already,) nor are we bound by our Office to attend to conversion of soules, and if any bee converted by us, it is accidentall.

In answer Welde wrote:

He strangely forgets himselfe, for 1. we say not that all our members are certainely reall Saints, but only visibly, so there may be some hypocrites amongst them, probably, that may neede conversion, and therefore by our Office we are to attend that worke as farre as the needs of the stocke shall appeare. 2. The children of our members (the charge of whom our Ministers undertake, even by vertue of their Offices) are not yet, haply, converted, and he is bound to fulfill his Office towards them.[40]

Puritan ministers apparently tried to convert two kinds of people: hypocrites who had been admitted to membership by mistake, and the children of the godly who enjoyed membership though not converted. Not a word about the mass of men who remained in the outer darkness![41]

An examination of Puritan sermons will establish the truth of Welde's unconscious revelation: New England ministers actually did devote their energy primarily to the "children of the church," not to the outside world. Thomas Hooker was the magnificent exception. Hooker remained in the seventeenth century as an example of evangelical zeal, a man who retained the original impulse of the Reformation, a man who spoke his words to sinners rather than saints. A glance at his writings will provide an illuminating contrast to those of other orthodox Puritan writers.[42] In his efforts at con-

[40] Thomas Welde, *An Answer to W. R.* (London, 1644), p. 58.

[41] On the Puritan concept of church membership and its implications, see Edmund S. Morgan, *Visible Saints: The History of a Puritan Idea* (New York, 1963).

[42] For Hooker was orthodox. His removal to Connecticut was the result of economic considerations, not of any disposition to quarrel with the monitors of

version he did not address himself only to the children of godly parents but to all sinners. He took advantage of the unregenerate audience with which the state provided him and directed many of his sermons at it. He spoke to men who had no godly parents to encourage them to seek God, men whose parents and friends rather would discourage them. "Now learne you to looke up to Christ," he said,

and looke to bee pittied by the Lord Jesus Christ. It may bee thy husband, or thy wife, or thy friends will not pittie thee, but will say, he is turned a precise fellow, and see now what good hee hath gotten by running to Sermons: thus they adde sorrow to sorrow, and persecution to persecution; because God hath smitten thee, therefore they smite thee too, but yet notwithstanding all this, looke thou up to the Lord Jesus Christ, and know that thou shalt finde favour; he will have a fellow-feeling with thee in all thy miseries. . . .[43]

Clearly Hooker was here addressing himself to men whose friends and relations were enemies of the Lord. He told them that to reach God they must fight against their relatives' opposition, for Christ

---

religion in the Bay. Throughout his life he remained in perfect accord with his fellow ministers, and his *Survey of the Summe of Church-Discipline* (London, 1648) became a standard handbook of the New England churches. Yet he admitted in that volume that he found it difficult to accept the doctrine which formed the theological basis of Puritan tribalism. He readily granted, with Calvin, that open and professed evildoers should be barred from the privileges of the church, but when it came to well-intentioned persons whose outward conduct showed no special vices, but who had never experienced conversion, he found it difficult to exclude such persons from the right to have their children baptized. "I shall nakedly professe," he said, "that if I should have given way to my affection, or followed that which suits my secret desire and inclination, I could have willingly wished, that the scale might have been cast upon the affirmative part, and that such persons (many whereof we hope are godly) might enjoy all such priviledges, which might be usefull and helpfull to them and theirs" (III, 11). For the sake of theological consistency Hooker restrained his affection and accepted the limitation of infant baptism to the children of the elect, but in his preaching he gave way to his "secret desire and inclination." On Hooker's orthodoxy see Perry Miller, "Thomas Hooker and the Democracy of Early Connecticut," *New England Quarterly*, IV, 663–712; and Morgan, *Visible Saints*, pp. 106–108.

[43] Thomas Hooker, *The Soules Exaltation*, p. 296.

came into the world to set *"The Father against the Son."* He told them that *"a mans Enemies shal be those of his own House,"* that "saving Grace sets them [the members of a family] in greatest opposition, and contrariety; and therefore must occasion the greatest contention amongst them."[44] As an example he cited Abraham's readiness to sacrifice his son Isaac. "This," said Hooker, "is that which God requireth not onely of *Abraham* but of all beleevers: *Whosoever will be my Disciple,* saith Christ, *must forsake father, and mother, and wife, and children, and houses, and lands; yea, and he must deny himselfe, and take up his Crosse, and follow me."*[45]

Hooker reached beyond the narrow bounds of the Puritan tribe; he preached his message to those who needed it most, those who had no godly parents to help and encourage them to seek God. Contrast with his expansiveness the attitude of other Puritan preachers. Thomas Cobbett addressed his book on the duties of children, not to all children, but to the children of proper descent. "Remember," he said, "I speak to the Children of the Godly, to the Children of the Church, though not altogether excluding others."[46] The kind of audience to which he and most other Puritan preachers directed their books and sermons is clearly revealed by the arguments with which they appealed for piety. Cobbett asked children to avoid sin not simply because sin was evil, but because

Hereby you become grossly unfaithfull, yea treacherous to your God, to your Ancestours, to your Parents, to posterity, to the whole Church. God made you his Trustees, and so did Ancestours and Parents make you their spirtuall Trustees, under God, to hold up Religion, Truth, the Worship, Waies, and Government of Christ, when they should be gathered to their Fathers; they look at and leave you their Children to be a seed of the Church, to be as *plants,* to hold up Gods *Orchards.*[47]

---

[44] *A Comment upon Christ's Last Prayer,* p. 416.
[45] *The Saints Dignitie and Dutie,* p. 168.
[46] Cobbett, *Frutifull and Usefull Discourse,* p. 59.
[47] Ibid., p. 197.

Such an argument must have left cold anyone whose parents and ancestors had not been members of the church. Similarly Eleazar Mather's *Serious Exhortation to the Present and Succeeding Generation in New England* was clearly addressed to the children of the godly only. In order to persuade his listeners to cleave unto God, he told them:

> *You have many special Engagements to hold God with you, he is your Fathers God, and not willing to leave you:* The holy Ghost gives counsel not to forsake our Fathers friend, much less *your Fathers God,* It's an heart endearing consideration that God was the God of Relations, this helps to sweeten the presence of God to us, as men in other things they will not part with what was their Progenitors, Oh this was my Fathers and I will not part with it: so here, he is a God left, commended and bequeathed to you by your Fathers....[48]

But God was not bequeathed to the children of the ungodly. These arguments were not designed to convert the mass of men but only the children of church members. Countless quotations could be produced to show that Puritan sermons proceeded by such arguments, which made no direct appeal to the unregenerate. Take for example the following invocation of genealogy in a sermon by William Stoughton:

> Consider and remember alwayes, that the *Books* that shall be opened at the last day will contain *Genealogies* in them. There shall then be brought forth a *Register of the Genealogies of New-Englands sons and daughters.* How shall we many of us hold up our faces then, when there shall be a solemn rehearsal of our *descent* as well as of our *degeneracies?* To have it published whose Child thou art will be cutting unto thy soul, as well as to have the Crimes reckoned up that thou art guilty of.[49]

Take, again, the argument which drew a picture of parent and child at the Day of Judgment. This was a favorite with many Puritan

---

[48] P. 30.

[49] William Stoughton, *New Englands True Interest, Not to Lie* (Cambridge, 1670), p. 33.

ministers, for it made the utmost of filial affection. Men should repent and become converted, it implied, because unless they did so,
they would be separated from their parents at the Last Day. "What
a dismal thing it will be," cried Increase Mather,

when a Child shall see his Father at the right Hand of Christ in the
day of Judgment, but himself at His left Hand: And when his
Father shall joyn with Christ in passing a Sentence of Eternal
Death upon him, saying, Amen O Lord, thou art Righteous in thus
Judging: And when after the Judgment, children shall see their
Father going with Christ to Heaven, but themselves going away
into Everlasting Punishment![50]

If the child of a saint was led by this reasoning to follow his father's
footsteps, the child of a sinner might have been led by the same
reasoning to follow *his* father's. Presumably filial affection would
make a child seek his parent's company in Hell as well as in Heaven.
Thomas Hooker, in contrast once again to other Puritans, took cog-
nizance of this fact in his appeals for conversion. His picture of the
Day of Judgment was painted from the standpoint of a sinful family, not a godly one, and its appeal was directed at religious feelings,
not at filial affection. Hooker warned his listeners precisely against
allowing their human affections to determine their conduct. "You
that are wives," he said,

and pretend that you must please your husbands, by submitting to
their commands and desires; you that are husbands, and alledge
that you must give satisfaction to your wives; you that are Apprentices, and plead, that if you observe not your masters wills, but
walk according to the rule of Gods word, you shall be thwarted by

---

[50] Increase Mather, *An Earnest Exhortation to the Children of New England
to Exalt the God of their Fathers* (Boston, 1711), p. 35. This argument was
especially favored by all the Mathers. For other examples see Eleazer Mather,
A Serious Exhortation, p. 31; Increase Mather, "Advice to the Children of
Godly Ancestors," in *A Course of Sermons on Early Piety,* pp. 12–13; Increase Mather, *The Duty of Parents to Pray for their Children* (Boston, 1719),
pp. 37–38; Increase Mather, *The Life and Death of that Reverend Man of
God, Mr. Richard Mather,* pp. 37–38; Cotton Mather, *Early Religion Urged,*
pp. 65–66.

your masters, and driven to some great inconvenience; You that stand upon the humoring of your friends and acquaintance, consider it well; will the perswasions, and counsels, and desires, and commands of a Father, or friend, or husband, or master, stand you in stead at the day of judgment? Will this be a satisfactorie answer at that day, my husband intreated me, my friends counselled me, my master commanded me? No, my brethren, as you are brethren in iniquitie, and causes of sin one to another, so you shall perish both together. Therefore knowing the terror of the Lord, let that scare you more then the anger and displeasure of all the friends in the world.[51]

The difference between Hooker's audience and Mather's is clear enough. Hooker was not talking to the children of saints.

Of course the other Puritan ministers did not devote themselves exclusively to church members and their children. Examples of evangelical preaching can be found in some of the works of almost all Puritan ministers. But such examples in the bulk of Puritan writing are comparatively rare. One example which in itself shows how thoroughly the tribal attitude gripped the most respected of Puritans may be found in John Cotton's book, *The Covenant of God's Free Grace*. After explaining the benefits of the covenant of grace to those who possessed it, Cotton paused to take the rest of the world into consideration. "But if a man be not entred into Christs Covenant," he asked, "how may hee enter into it, or if he be, how may he know it?" Cotton answered the question simply and without equivocation:

For the answer of this, consider with your self, whether any of your ancestors have been under this Covenant, yea or no; if they have, whether then have you renounced this Covenant, or laid claim to it? If you can say, you have known some of your ancestors in this Covenant, and you have not refused it, but laid claim unto it, when you understood yourselves, it is a certain signe this Covenant reacheth to you, for the Covenant of God is, *I will be thy God, and the God of thy seed after thee.*

[51] *The Saints Dignitie and Dutie,* p. 147.

But how if I know not whether any of my ancestors were good or no, what must I do then that I may be under the Covenant?

For the answer of this, consider, have you not lived in some good families? it is a great stay to you if you have, for this reacheth to all; the Covenant is made to the housholders and their servants: *Abraham* circumcised all his house by vertue of this, *I am a God to thee, and to thy seed.* So that unlesse they have abrogated this Covenant, it followeth them still, and they may claim it to themselves.

But how if neither of the former I can challenge to my self; but all that I have had to deal withall have been carnall men, what may I do in such a case to get within the Covenant?

I confesse then thy condition is so much the more to be pitied; but seeing we were not born free, wee must therefore take a course whereby wee may become free....

If you be not in the Covenant, but your whole desire is, that you may, you must labour to bring yourselves into a good family....[52]

An avenue by which to enter the Covenant was thus left to poor sinners: they could get into a good family, as servants or by marriage. But Cotton did not stop to press the point—nor did he or any other Puritan minister return to it at greater length in any other place. Rather the ministers did their best to make it difficult for an unregenerate man to enter a godly family. They advised the masters of families not to hire ungodly servants lest their children be corrupted by contagion,[53] and they condemned all marriages in which church members were yoked to the unregenerate. When the children of the godly showed a propensity for picking mates from the ranks of the reprobate, Increase Mather warned the parents that their descendants would ultimately be cut off from God's favor. "Take heed," he admonished,

how you dispose of your Children ... It may make us dread to think what's coming, in that it is with us as it was with the old World, the Sons of God are marrying with the Daughters of men,

[52] John Cotton, *The Covenant of Gods free Grace*, pp. 19–20.
[53] Cotton Mather, *A Good Master well Served*, p. 9.

Church Members in disposing of their Children look more at Portion than at Piety . . . a sad sign that Religion will expire, and such Families be cut off from the Covenant, within a few Generations, and the branches thereof perish for ever.[54]

All the odds, therefore, were against the unregenerate. They were brought to church, but they were not preached to. They were told to get into a godly family, but the doors to such families were closed wherever the ministers could close them.

The Puritans had a neat theological explanation for this neglect of the mass of men. The argument was simple: comparatively few people are saved anyhow, and those who are almost always belong to the same families. Given two generations, the persons who are saved in the second generation will almost invariably be the children of those who were saved in the first. The children of the saints in one generation will be the saints of the next. The church, therefore, in neglecting a large proportion of the population neglects very few potential saints. The most likely candidates for conversion are the children of church members. As the Puritans usually stated the idea, "God casts the line of election in the loins of godly parents." This phrase became one of the clichés of Puritan preaching. Take for example the works of Increase Mather, "the foremost American Puritan." In 1678 he was telling it to the congregation at the Old South Church in Boston; John Hull copied his words in a notebook: "god casts the line of election to run very much in those that are of elect Parents."[55] That same year Mather published a treatise entitled *Pray for the Rising Generation*, in which he announced: "Now God hath seen meet to cast the line of Election so, as that it

[54] Increase Mather, "A Discourse concerning the Danger of Apostasy," in *A Call from Heaven*, pp. 128–129. Cf. the statement approved by the synod of 1680: "It is lawful for all sorts of people to marry, who are able with judgment to give their consent. Yet it is the duty of Christians to marry in the Lord; and, therefore, such as profess the true reformed religion should not marry with infidels, papists, or other idolaters: Neither should such as are godly be unequally yoked, by marrying such as are wicked in their life, or maintain damnable heresie." (Cotton Mather, *Magnalia*, II, 202.)

[55] Boston Sermons, July 3, 1678.

doth (though not wholly and only, yet) for the most part run through the loyns of godly parents. . . . And there are some Families that the Lord hath Chosen above others and therefore poureth his Spirit upon the Offspring in such Families successively."⁵⁶ The next year he published a sermon entitled *A Call from Heaven to the Present and Succeeding Generation in New England.* Once more he disclosed:

Tho it be not wholly and only so, that Elect Parents have none but elect Children, or that elect children are alwaies born of elect Parents yet God hath seen meet to cast the line of election so, as that generally elect Children are cast upon elect Parents. . . . There are some Families in the world, that God hath designed to shew peculiar mercy to them, from generation to generation. And if an account should be taken concerning all the godly men that are now alive in the world, doubtless it would be found that the greatest part of them are sprung from godly Parents.⁵⁷

In 1703 Mather again labored the point in a tract called *The Duty of Parents to Pray for their Children:* "Experience has confirmed this Truth, that Grace is most ordinarily given to the Children that are sprung from Godly Parents . . . If there should be a strict Trial made concerning it throughout the World at this day, without doubt it would be found that the greatest part of Godly men on the face of the Earth are such as were born of Godly Parents."⁵⁸ Two years before his death Mather was still saying it: "Some well Observed, God has so cast the *Line of Election* that for the most part it runs through the Loins of *Godly Parents.* . . . Doubtless, if an account of it were taken, it would be found that the *greatest part* of such as belong to God have descended from *Godly Parents.*"⁵⁹

This notion was no idiosyncrasy of Increase Mather. Quotations

---

⁵⁶ Increase Mather, *Pray for the Rising Generation* (Cambridge, 1678), p. 178.

⁵⁷ *A Call from Heaven*, pp. 7, 9.

⁵⁸ *The Duty of Parents to Pray for their Children*, pp. 14–15.

⁵⁹ "Advice to the Children of Godly Ancestors," in *A Course of Sermons on Early Piety*, pp. 5–6.

to the same purport could be taken from other Puritan writers.[60]
The idea sprang from the promise God made to Abraham, namely,
that he would save Abraham's family and descendants, as well as
himself. The Puritans extended this promise from Abraham to
every believer. It doubtless brought great comfort to know that you
belonged to a family which had been given special privileges by the
Lord. It reduced to a minimum the uncertainty of living under an
omnipotent and arbitrary God, for it meant that if your father was
saved, you would probably be saved too, and so would your children. Even if children showed no visible signs of grace, there was
still good reason to believe that they would finally be saved.

Suppose you have seen your *Ungodly Children* Dy before you,
without Evident Marks of a *Saving Change* upon them: However
still Hope the best. A famous man would say, *If I see a Child that
hath either a Godly Father, or a Godly Mother, I shall have Hope
for Him a Long while: But if he has a Godly Father and Mother
too, I'le never leave Hoping for him, till I see him Turn'd off the
Gallows.* Who can tell, what the *Grace* of God may have done for
them, in their Last Minutes? It may be, *Between the Stirrup and
the Ground.* Yea, and if *They* should be *Lost,* who can tell, what
the Lord may do for the *Third Generation.* Tho' the *Son* of *Samuel*
were not as he should be, yet his *Grand Son* was a most Notable
Prophet of the Lord.[61]

The idea was especially comforting when children died in infancy:

You may be satisfied concerning your *Children* Departed in their
Infancy, *That the Alsufficient God, will according to His Promise,
be a God unto them, throughout Eternal Ages.* My Brethren, This
Blessing of Abraham is *come upon* you, by the Lord Jesus Christ.
You may inscribe upon their Gravestone, that *Epitaph,* OF
SUCH IS THE KINGDOM OF HEAVEN: or that *Epitaph,* RE-
SERVED FOR A GLORIOUS RESURRECTION: or that *Epi-
taph,* GONE, BUT NOT LOST.[62]

[60] Cf. Cotton Mather, *Help for Distressed Parents,* pp. 12–13; Eleazar
Mather, *A Serious Exhortation,* pp. 18–19; Thomas Thatcher, Boston Sermons,
August 19, 1677.
    [61] Cotton Mather, *Help for Distressed Parents,* pp. 34–35.
    [62] Ibid., p. 38.

No matter how reassuring such doctrines may have been to the godly parent, they lacked visible confirmation in the history of the church. In spite of their theological advantages and in spite of all the preaching directed at them, the children did not get converted, either before they came of age or after. God refused to become a respecter of persons. He refused to grant a monopoly on salvation to a religious elite. As a result the number of full members in the churches gradually shrank until the ecclesiastical structure could no longer hold together. The Half-Way Covenant of 1662 enabled the unconverted children of church members to retain their incomplete membership after becoming adults, but it did not increase the number of full communicants. Before the end of the century the Puritan system was tottering.

The founders of New England had staked the success of their experiment on the success of their churches. They confined political rights to church members, so that the existence of the state depended upon the maintenance of a continuous supply of converts for the churches. If the supply failed, not only the church but the state, too, would collapse, for a kingdom of God could not be maintained without the support of godly citizens. The Puritan system failed because the Puritans relied upon their children to provide the church with members and the state with citizens. Even when it became apparent that their children were not up to the task, they did not take the obvious step of looking for material elsewhere. Instead they intensified the campaign to win the children; they wrote, they preached, they prayed, they threatened—but to no avail. It did not lie in their power to give the final ecstatic experience of grace without which true devotion must prove impossible. After they had exercised all the means of grace, they had to leave the issue with God, and long before the end of the century God's answer had become unmistakable. Though Increase Mather was still mumbling his phrases about the loins of godly parents in 1721, it was long since clear, to anyone with eyes to see, that grace was not hereditary.

The Puritans had, in fact, committed the very sin that they so often admonished themselves to avoid: they had allowed their children to usurp a higher place than God in their affections. Like

Adam, they had upset the order of creation, had placed love of the creature above the demands of the Creator. To be sure, other forces than tribalism had also betrayed them: they had grown prosperous and comfortable, and prosperity had proved as always an enemy to zeal. But other failings only compounded the sin of insubordination to a God for whom their fathers had defied prelacy and privilege. When theology became the handmaid of genealogy, Puritanism no longer deserved its name.

Index